Politics, Economics and Investments

Don's Thoughts

Donald M. Kinzer

authorHOUSE®

AuthorHouse™ LLC
1663 Liberty Drive
Bloomington, IN 47403
www.authorhouse.com
Phone: 1-800-839-8640

Published by AuthorHouse   05/13/2014

ISBN: 978-1-4969-1263-3 (sc)
ISBN: 978-1-4969-1262-6 (e)

To My Beloved Katie Girl
From Dad

Contents

Preface

This book discusses financial trends in terms of the overall economy, the U.S. political process, and the investment prospects currently and projected into the future.

Chapter One deals with the current financial and economic trends in the United States. These trends regarding the deficit and the Federal Reserve's massive bond purchase program are not sustainable. Further, the Federal Reserve's program establishes a new frontier in monetary policy which is a major experiment without a predictable outcome.

In the next chapter, I will argue that globalization has fundamentally changed economic growth and employment prospects for the U.S., Western Europe, and Japan. The U.S. has lost more than 10 million manufacturing jobs in the past 30 years. Virtually all of these are permanent losses. The lack of emphasis on globalization's impact on the U.S. and other advanced countries is difficult for me to comprehend. I will offer my explanation of why globalization is such an economic force and why it gets so little attention in the U.S. media.

Chapter Three discusses asset bubbles which have occurred since 1970 and Chapter Four addresses the housing bubble specifically. Asset bubbles have occurred throughout history. During the late 1960s, Keynesian oriented economists, such as Paul Samuelson, believed that bubbles were a thing of the past. In fact, they believed that with the proper application of Keynesian economics, even business cycles could be eliminated. However, we have experienced a series of extraordinary bubbles with first, the commodities bubble of the 1970s, then the commercial real estate bubble of the late 1980s, then the stock market bubble of the late 1990s, and finally the housing bubble which burst in 2008. Bubbles contribute to economic growth when they are inflating, and tend to cause recessions when they burst. These four bubbles have punctuated the economy since the 1970s. Currently, we have the possibility of another bubble occurring in the bond market, as the Federal Reserve holds interest rates at artificially low levels and governments worldwide are running significant operating deficits.

Chapters Five and Six deal with the financial problems from the standpoint of the two political parties: first with the Republicans and then with the Democrats. The first graph in Chapter One shows the revenue of approximately 15% of GDP and expenses of approximately 24% of GDP. These points are about equidistant from the 19-20% average federal expenditures and tax revenue versus GDP which we have had since World War II. Republicans characterize the problem as a "spending problem, not a taxing problem," and the Democrats believe that further increases in spending are necessary to stimulate economic growth. I believe the truth is somewhere in the middle and that both spending cuts and increased revenue will be necessary to bring the deficit down to a manageable size. This will be further complicated by the slower pace of economic growth caused by the globalization trends.

Chapter Seven deals with investments and how they are impacted by economic and political trends. And finally Chapter Eight deals with the energy revolution now occurring in the U.S.; one of the most positive areas of potential growth in 2013 and beyond.

Chapter Nine are some conclusions I have reached. They are not all inclusive; and they do not solve all the world's problems. Moreover, they are suggestions for the President to consider as he tries to manage the problems of the world.

Foreword

This book was Don's last project. Don completed it as his Parkinson's disease continued to progress. He began by writing down his thoughts, but most of the book was dictated and transcribed by Judi Pinckney, a loyal associate. Don wanted very much to see it published.

The book is a collection of Don's thoughts on the economy, politics, and the financial markets. It is pure Don Kinzer. The book relates personal experiences, conversations, observations, and just plain thoughts on many different topics. Most importantly, the book encompasses Don's career as a professional investor and a Chief Financial Officer for a regional bank and for an insurance company, and as a private investor for his personal portfolio.

Don was convinced that globalization, which started with the fall of the Berlin Wall was the primary cause for the slow worldwide GDP growth. He was convinced it is the primary cause of the economic problems of the western world (Western Europe, England, and the United States). Don did not see an early resolution to the globalization issue and felt it would be a long, long time before the western world experienced above average GDP growth again.

Don was also convinced there was a worldwide bond bubble building that would have severe consequences. He felt the impact on individual investor's fixed income investments would be devastating.

Don's views on politics were quite strong. He blamed both parties for the economic mess we have been in. Neither the Republicans nor the Democrats are facing reality with the demands they each propose in Congress. It is very much a Mexican standoff with no easy resolution.

Finally, Don finishes with some ideas of how to better our current economic and financial situation. He by no means says he has all the answers, but has good food for thought.

Don was a beloved friend, confidant, tennis buddy, party associate, and many other wonderful relationships. I miss him very much.

Now to read Don's thoughts—its' time to begin his labor of love.

Peter Dawyot

Chapter One

The Current
Unsustainable Situation

Before 2009, the budget deficit of the United States was being funded by foreign countries with which we have a negative balance of payments: primarily Japan, Saudi Arabia, and China. Now it is primarily being funded by the Federal Reserve. The Fed is buying 80+% of new U.S. Treasury debt issued. Perhaps this change was caused because the countries were getting imbalanced on Treasury securities in their investments. Regardless, it has allowed the Federal Reserve to reduce interest rates to historically low levels. Moreover, it has allowed the Federal Reserve to maintain a very loose monetary policy since 2009.

"The American people have spoken: they don't want their benefits reduced and they don't want their taxes increased." So said a *New York Times* analyst summing up the 2012 election. However, there's one major problem with this position: it resulted in a deficit of almost $1 trillion as shown in the graph below. In 2009, federal expenditures exceeded 25% of GDP, the highest since World War II. Revenues (taxes), on the other hand, were below 15%, the lowest since World War II. While some improvement has occurred since then, the country's budget is still in deficit. The spread to GDP is now 4% vs. 10% in 2009.

A deficit of almost $600 billion is still projected for 2014. In Obama's first term, deficits totaled almost $5 trillion, producing a 50% increase in the national debt. Of course, much of this debt build up was inherited from the financial crisis, which occurred in the last year of the Bush (43) Administration. This has been the slowest economic recovery in the post-World War II period and unemployment remains extraordinarily high. The graph below illustrates the Federal Governments' expenses and revenues for the last 80 years.

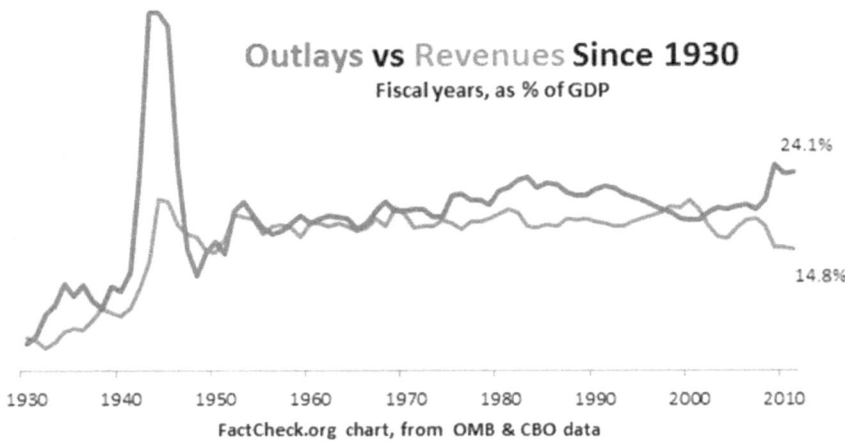

While we tend to blame the Congress or the Obama Administration or Washington in general for this problem, two recent surveys make it clear that the problem is more pervasive. In the first survey, over 75% of responders said that government spending was out of control and must be reined in. However, a second survey reflected that more than 80% of the people said that entitlements should not be reduced. As the preeminent American philosopher, Pogo Possum, stated "I have met the enemy and they are us."

The current situation: historically high deficits and historically low interest rates

A deficit of the magnitude of the current deficit would ordinarily cause interest rates to go up, or the dollar to decline in value versus other currencies, or both. But these are not ordinary times. Because of globalization, virtually all of the advanced economies went into recession in 2008. Europe is still in recession and Japan has had no economic growth for several decades. Consequently, the dollar is seen as the strongest currency among the major world economies.

And U.S. interest rates, despite the deficit, are at historic lows. The yield on ten-year Treasury notes is below 3%. The current 30-year fixed rate mortgage rate of 3.5% is the lowest in history. The Federal Reserve is holding interest rates extremely low to increase economic growth and reduce unemployment. However, one unintended consequence of this is that the Fed is aiding and abetting the lack of progress in tackling the deficit situation by Congress and the Obama Administration.

The Federal Reserve hopes to increase the pace of economic growth and to bring the unemployment rate down to 6.5% from the current rate of 7.7%. In this pursuit, the Federal Reserve has increased their balance sheet from $1 trillion to $3 trillion, and it will be approximately $4 trillion at the end of 2013. The unprecedented size of the fiscal deficits and the unprecedented increase in the size of the balance sheet of the Federal Reserve are experiments without historical references to predict the ultimate consequences. The longer they persist the more difficult it will be to contain the consequences.

Deficits do matter

Dick Cheney, while Vice President of the United States, stated to the Secretary of the Treasury, Paul O'Neill, that "deficits don't matter, Reagan proved that." And on the other end of the political spectrum liberal Democrats, such as columnist Paul Krugman, have advocated higher deficits in the current period to increase the pace of economic activity.

However, deficits do matter. If, for example, the total U.S. debt reaches 100% of GDP and interest rates normalize to 5%, then the interest rate cost of the debt would be 5% of GDP. Keep in mind that total federal spending has been approximately 20% of GDP since World War II. With this increased borrowing cost plus the increased costs of entitlement expenditures, we are looking at a significant increase in the federal expenditures versus GDP. When federal spending takes up a larger proportion of our economic activity, the pace of economic activity will be reduced and this will limit the response to future economic crises.

The consequences of Federal Reserve activity

The dollar has remained relatively strong because the currencies of most other advanced economies are performing as badly or worse than the U.S. And, interest rates are being held artificially low by the Federal Reserve.

This leaves the critics of deficit spending with a fairly weak argument that we are leaving our problems and pain for future generations.

Even assuming that the Federal Reserve's monetary easing policies do not end in a disaster, we have entered into a new era, with the purchase of debt securities by the Federal Reserve having long term consequences. Just as the tendency of each administration is to operate with a deficit, the tendency will be to lobby the Fed to purchase securities to hold interest rates down.

Ben Bernanke, the former Chairman of the Federal Reserve, says he sleeps well, unless his little dog, who sleeps with him, gets restless during the night. There are several reasons why he should not sleep well.

First, by holding interest rates so low, he is in effect allowing the federal government to operate at huge deficits. Even with the improving economy and the completion of the stimulus program, we nonetheless have deficits of some $700 billion per year. This is still far greater than any deficit run prior to 2008.

Secondly, the wrong people are going to get hurt when interest rates normalize. In 401Ks, for example, there are usually no money market alternatives, and the Treasury option is viewed as the safe "risk free" option. However, if 10-year Treasury yields go up just 2 percentage points to 4%, they will decrease the price of the bond by 18% ($1000 to $820). If yields go to 5%, which is close to the long term average, the value declines 25%. Most people do not realize the risk of this reduced valuation.

Further, many 401Ks have an option which adjusts automatically to changes in age. This formula emphasizes growth stocks when someone is young, and increasingly relies on value oriented stocks and bonds as one gets older. Many have 50-60% invested in bonds when someone is near retirement. Thus, the sector which advisors consider the lowest risk actually has a much higher risk than stocks.

Mr. Bernanke has been very forthright and explicit that what he is trying to do is to increase jobs. This is part of the dual mandate of the Federal Reserve of the United States. Other central banks, such as European Central Bank (ECB), are only charged with the responsibility for holding prices stable. Further, he said that he does not like the idea of having the Chairman of the Federal Open Market Committee (FOMC) having a status where decisions are viewed as his rather than the committee's. This is no doubt a reference to his predecessor, Alan Greenspan, who increasingly spoke as if he were the Federal Reserve.

But he must show more concern for the implications of this low interest rate strategy. And, of greater concern are the implications of the purchase of $1 trillion per year of long term mortgage and U.S. Treasury debt. In addition to the examples listed above, money has flowed into the stock market which is now trading at all-time highs. More worrisome, as investors search for yield, a rally has occurred in so-called junk bonds, securities issued by companies that are below investment grade.

It's different this time

Economists warn against using the phrase "it's different this time" to describe the period of excess in one sector of the economy or another. For example, the stock market bubble in the late 1990s was justified based on "new paradigms" related to the price of internet stocks.

However, every recession has some degree of cyclicality and some degree of structural change. The impact of globalization, plus technology advancements, and the aging of the population all make this particular recession more difficult to escape than previous recessions. Media commentators continue to emphasize the cyclical nature of the recession. However, I believe this is primarily because of the structural aspects. This is why we cannot use the traditional responses to end high unemployment this cycle. So in the current debate, Democrats tend to emphasize the traditional fiscal stimulus programs in order to increase jobs. In the next chapter, I'll make the case that globalization has changed the traditional relationships to the point that the traditional goal of 5.5% unemployment is not realistic. I believe the Federal Reserve recognizes this since they set 6.5% as the goal of the current quantitative easing program.

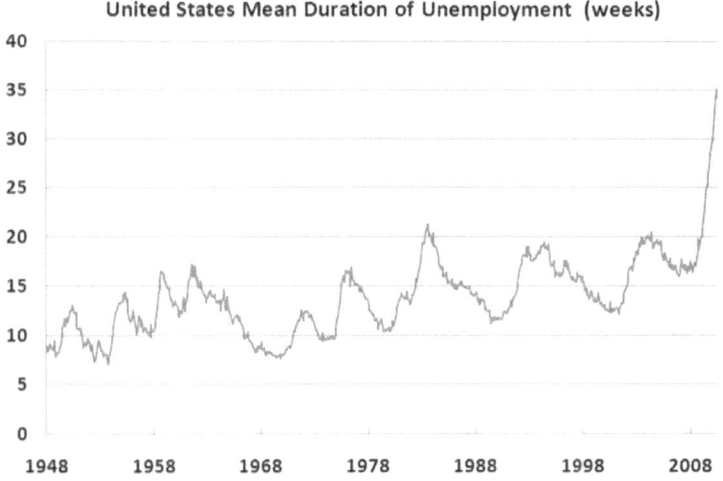

While I believe the subpar growth in the economy will continue, the good news is that the economy could grow for some time. Historically, periods of economic growth have only lasted for four to five years before being interrupted by a recession. But this time, we could see a long, slow recovery, with the growth generated by the energy sector, the federal deficit (which is forecast to average around $500 billion over the coming years), and the low interest rates that are being produced by the Federal Reserve. While these last two causes of stimulus to economic growth are not sustainable on a long term basis, they nonetheless can, and probably will, stimulate some economic growth over the short term.

The Federal Reserve must police asset bubbles

When bubbles occur in the economy, the administration in power will not recognize them, but rather will cheer them on. The Clinton Administration cheered on the technology bubble (Al Gore claimed to be the father of the internet). The Bush (43) Administration cheered on the housing bubble claiming that it was part of a new "ownership society." And the Obama Administration would not comment on the artificially low interest rates which have likely created a bubble in the bond market.

This leaves only the Federal Reserve to attempt to police asset bubbles. It is ironic, however, that the housing bubble was actually championed by Federal Reserve Chairman, Alan Greenspan. As I will discuss in a subsequent chapter regarding asset bubbles, Mr. Greenspan produced a low interest rate environment which bred the housing bubble. Further, his policy of increased self-regulation of the banking system allowed the subprime mortgage bubble to go undetected. Third, he denied that a housing bubble was occurring. He repeatedly said that while home prices were somewhat "frothy," they were "well contained." Some commentators have theorized that he wanted the economy to be growing rapidly when he retired, to cap his tenure as the "greatest central banker in the history of the world."

As stated before, I don't believe Bernanke is on an ego trip. I believe he is genuinely concerned about the high level of unemployment and is attempting an experiment with unorthodox Federal Reserve practices in order to reduce unemployment.

How will the Federal Reserve's policies play out?

At this point it is difficult to tell how the Fed's policies will eventually work out. I will attempt to describe the possibilities in four scenarios.

Scenario number one: The economy grows rapidly and the 6.5 unemployment is achieved relatively quickly. This would enable the Federal Reserve to significantly reduce their current purchase of $85 billion per month of long-term government bonds and mortgages.

Scenario number two: Inflation becomes a problem and the Fed is forced to reduce or abandon their quantitative easing program.

Scenario number three: Some negative economic shock occurs, such as major dissolution of the Euro monetary system, which produces an economic recession and causes a total rethinking of the Fed's approach.

Scenario number four: Continued slow economic recovery. This scenario implies that interest rates will be held low until at least 2015 and bond purchases would continue for at least another year.

I believe this fourth scenario is the most likely to occur. In a globalized world, I do not believe any advanced economy will be able to achieve the rapid economic growth of the past 40 years. Japan has had subpar growth for 30 years. European economies have suffered with subpar growth and are currently in a double dip recession. The attempts to stimulate the pace of economic activity have not worked out well. Housing prices in the U.S. is the most vivid example, and this type of stimulus was also attempted in several European countries. Spain, for example, had an even larger bubble in housing and their housing crash has resulted in an unemployment rate of 27%.

The second scenario of higher inflation would result only if debt was increased significantly. More importantly, the globalized economy has available labor resources which seem likely to prevent a wage price spiral which occurred in the 1970s in the U.S.

Scenario three: a negative shock in Europe or China is certainly possible and difficult to predict.

The problem with inequality

There is another major problem that we must recognize: economic growth has been skewed toward the very wealthy. Some people are even questioning whether or not capitalism can produce equal treatment. In his excellent heartfelt book, *Who Stole the American Dream?*, Hedrick Smith contends that both Washington's policies and the practices of America's business leaders are responsible for the decline of the middle class.

In *Foreign Affairs* magazine, Jerry Muller has an excellent essay on capitalism and inequality.

Let me state that I think there is a sharp contrast between the reasons why the Federal Reserve is currently holding down interest rates under the Chairmanship of Bernanke versus that of his predecessor. Mr. Bernanke is clearly attempting to reduce unemployment without creating inflation, which are the goals of the Federal Reserve. He has been extremely open in describing the Fed's efforts, and has allowed thorough questioning by analysts in the media at press conferences subsequent to each open market decision meeting.

In contrast, I believe Alan Greenspan, in his later years, became so intellectually arrogant that he did not recognize the possibility of failure and consequently helped to propel the U.S. economy and the world economy into one of the worst crisis that has occurred since World War II.

In this book I will describe why I think globalization has impacted the economy in more profound ways than most politicians and most economists will admit. I believe globalization has resulted in lower levels of employment and growth in the economies of the Europe, England, Japan, and the U.S.

The slow pace of recovery in the U.S., Europe, and Japan does have one advantage: it could lead to a long recovery. Having already lasted for four years, it could last for another three to four years without a recession because the financial and consumption excesses which invariably build up in periods of faster economic growth.

However, in the U.S. we simply cannot continue the excessive debt creation, whether funded by China and other foreign countries or funded by the Federal Reserve, without producing a bubble which will have very negative consequences.

The current period of hyper-partisanship in D.C. does not produce an atmosphere where solutions can be easily found. Both parties are advocating policies which will simply not work in the current environment. For the Republican Party to advocate reduced tax rates when the budget deficit is 40% of government spending is simply unrealistic. And, for Democrats to advocate increased government spending at even higher deficit levels is just as unrealistic.

We need to recognize that a lower growth of economic activity is likely for the coming years and adjust our thinking to that new reality. This book suggests that asset bubbles which have punctuated our economy for the past 40 years will continue. Such bubbles were once thought not to be a part of a modern economy. And, yet, we have had one asset bubble after another for the past four decades. I will suggest certain investment principles which I believe are appropriate for the economy for some years to come. This is not an investment textbook, but, I will describe some common sense investment ideas which I think will be prudent and will make money in the coming economic environment. Throughout the book I have one major concern for the U.S. economy: that the current level of deficits and increases in debt being financed primarily by the World Central Bank is unsustainable. This is the primary area of excess that exists today. The Federal Reserve and other central banks, including the Bank of Japan, the Bank of England, and the European Central Bank are at risk of producing a debt bubble which will ultimately crash their respective economies. This is by far the major danger in the world today.

Alternative ending for chapter one

How is it possible that in the last four years that we could have a federal government running record budget deficits and yet have record low interest rates on Treasury bonds and mortgages? These conditions would ordinarily cause interest rates to spike higher and the dollar to decline dramatically. But those who warn about the problem with such huge deficits are quick to say that we are relegating our debt to succeeding generations. They cannot point to either inflation or to a U.S. dollar decline, nor to higher interest rates as being a result of the current federal deficit.

To understand how this can occur, we have to take a look at conditions in other countries. The European economy generally is worse than the U.S. although it varies markedly from country to country.

The Japanese economy has never recovered from the asset bubble that was created in the late 1980s. To get some idea of how strong this bubble was, the Nikkei average exceeded 40,000 points in 1989. Currently, the Nikkei average is 15,000 points after 35 years.

As always, there was a rationale for this tremendous bubble. The Japanese economy was by any measure the strongest economy in the world at the time. And more importantly, the Japanese economy has seen zero growth in the past 35 years. Economists have varying explanations for why there has been so little growth in the Japanese economy. I believe it is primarily because of globalization and, the rise of China primarily, and secondarily, to the rise of Taiwan and South Korea as competitors. There are certainly other factors, including demographics that contribute to this lack of growth, but again I believe the primary cause was globalization, and the rise of China's economy.

So we end up with the dollar being the strongest large currency in the world. While the currencies of Australia, New Zealand, Canada, and Switzerland are among currencies which are stronger, they do not have the size to compete with the U.S. dollar.

As the interest rates remain low despite the deficit spending, for some years it was because of China, Japan, Saudi Arabia and other countries buying U.S. Treasury securities which were created to finance the deficit. More recently, it has been primarily the Federal Reserve purchasing the Treasury securities. These purchases of mortgage and Treasury securities are approximately $1 trillion per year. Federal Reserve Chairman Bernanke was best noted academically for his studies of the Great Depression in the U.S. He believed that the Federal Reserve and federal government should have done more to spur economic growth, and protect the economy from deflation which occurred in the 1930s. Further, he is very mindful of the fact that the federal government attempted to balance the budget too early in 1938 when it can be argued that the economy was still coming out of the depression.

Consequently he has been very diligent in efforts to prevent deflation and to seek economic growth and reduce unemployment. With no price inflation evident, the Fed has paid special attention to its other mandate: to create the maximum level of employment.

Alternative ending for chapter one

My theory on the subpar performance of the U.S. economy differs from what John Maynard Keynes called the "conventional wisdom" in one important respect: I believe globalization is having a far bigger impact on economic growth potential of all advanced countries to a much greater extent than do the political commentators or political economists. I will explain in Chapter 2 why this is the case, and will provide some theories as to why politicians and public economists do not agree.

The reason this is so important is that, if I am correct, if globalization has reduced the economic growth prospects in advanced countries, then many governments and central banks are trying to do something which is not a realistic possibility. That includes the current U.S. government and the Federal Reserve Board.

The GOP claims that economic growth is being slowed by the actions of the federal government, including regulations, etc., and that reducing the size of government would free the economy to expand.

The Democrats, on the other hand, claim that the economy's stimulus, however as shown in the first graph in Chapter One, the Republicans should be getting enough stimulus since the cost of government is well below what it has been for the past few years and the Democrats should be getting stimulus because the costs are well above what they have been. In ordinary times this would produce a significantly higher rate of interest and/or decline in the value of the dollar but these are not ordinary times.

Let me state from the outset that I am not a "China basher." I believe the impact of globalization has been extraordinary. The fact that over a half billion people have been moved from sub-poverty to above the poverty line in China alone is a graphic illustration of the benefits of globalization. However, the introduction of hundreds of millions of people who work for wages far below those in advanced countries means that the impact on the middle class and on the overall economies of those advanced countries will be decidedly negative.

At a press conference subsequent to the March, 2013 Federal Reserve meeting, Mr. Bernanke was asked if he thought any bubbles were occurring in the economy. Mr. Bernanke immediately discussed the stock market and the fact that valuations are not out of line compared with earnings. He pointed out that on an inflation adjusted basis the stock market had not gone up nearly as much as it had in nominal terms. It did not seem to occur to him that the bubble was in fact in bonds and those bond prices were being influenced or inflated by the Federal Reserve.

But as I have said before, the Federal Reserve <u>must</u> be on guard for asset bubbles. The administration in power is ordinarily so growth-oriented that it does the necessary policing because bursting the bubbles would necessarily reduce the pace of economic activity. Consequently, we could not expect the Clinton Administration to address the bubble in technology stocks nor the Bush (43) Administration to address the unsustainable pace of home building nor the Obama Administration to address the low interest rates. The Federal Reserve is the only institution capable of making these tough decisions which would reduce economic activity. The Federal Reserve has not done so for a variety of reasons.

Alan Greenspan famously said that subsequent to the technology bubble that the Federal Reserve should not intervene in an asset bubble, but rather should just be around to pick up the pieces when the bubble burst. This is not what I would expect from the Federal Reserve.

The President of the New York Federal Reserve, William Dudley, said in a speech in 2009, that the Central Bank should deal with bubbles in a variety of ways. First, they should use the "bully pulpit" of the Federal Reserve to warn of the bubble occurring. Then they should check to determine if banking regulations are adequate to address the bubble as it is occurring. And third, if all else fails, they should increase interest rates to prevent the bubble from growing too risky proportions.

Alan Greenspan chose not to deal with asset bubbles. In the housing crisis, he set the stage for the bubble by keeping interest rates too low for too long. Rather than warn of the bubble, he proclaimed that while housing prices were somewhat high, this situation in total was "well contained." Further, his emphasis on "self-regulation" on Wall Street freed the banks to pursue activities which increased the risk of the housing collapse.

And now Bernanke is pursuing policies to increase economic activity and reduce unemployment. But in so doing, he is creating artificially low prices in bonds which must ultimately be brought back to more normal levels. Whether or not this is a bubble will depend on the severity of the economic consequences when interest rates are normalized. At any rate, with the very best of intentions, we are likely seeing a bubble being created which will ultimately have to be burst with the reduction of economic activity.

Alternative wording

Even in the best of circumstances Mr. Bernanke has introduced an alternative which will have the potential for misuse later on. Just as the stimulus measures in the fiscal budget, as advocated by a Keynesian economist, have been much more politically acceptable than the alternative of a balanced budget, so too will the prospect of quantitative easing be more politically palatable in the future. The combination of federal deficit spending by the Treasury and bond purchase by the Federal Reserve seems like a proverbial "free lunch." Which brings us back to the Milton Freidman maxim that" there is no free lunch."

Alternative wording

First, the bursting of the commercial property bubble in 1991 caused a recession. Then, the bursting of the technology bubble in 2000 also caused a recession. And finally, as the Obama Administration is so quick to point out on any occasion, the bursting of the housing bubble in 2007 caused the most severe recession since the Great Depression. Obviously, no administration wants a recession and it is always difficult to tell when a bubble is occurring. In fact, of note earlier, the Clinton Administration cheered on the technology bubble and the Bush (43) Administration cheered on the "ownership society."

In the press conference following the March FOMC meeting, Chairman Bernanke said that the Fed had indeed set up procedures to search for any bubble that was being created. He said this in response to a question about bubbles that were occurring and he immediately referenced the stock market as not representing a bubble because the earnings were good, growth was good, and so forth. However, he seemed oblivious to the prospect of a bond bubble. This is in keeping with the history of bubbles—no one recognizes them while they are occurring.

Media frequently cite the low level of interest rates as an indicator that the deficit is not a problem. Frequently, commentators on MSNBC laugh at the notion that high deficits are a problem when interest rates are at historical lows.

Rogoff states that the cause of asset bubbles is human nature. This implies that they will recur again and again and also that they are in need of more attention and emphasis by the Federal Reserve. As stated in Chapter One, the Federal Reserve is the only independent source to combat bubbles.

Alan Greenspan is now working on a book for release in October 2013; a portion of which is related to the weakness of "human nature." I suppose this will be the missing "glitch" in his model. Again, causing the housing bubble to be much more severe than it otherwise would have been by insisting repeatedly that it was "well contained." The current President of the New York Federal Reserve, William C. Dudley, stated that the Fed should do three things to combat bubbles: use the bully pulpit of the Chairman's position to warn of bubbles, enforce regulations to combat bubbles, and to raise interest rates as a last resort. Mr. Greenspan violated all three by keeping interest rates too low for too long, pursuing a "self-regulation" policy on Wall Street, and insisting that the problem was well-contained.

I would add to the human nature explanation by Ken Rogoff that politics is also a formidable cause of bubbles and also perpetuates the bubbles. Again, the Clinton Administration would not have criticized the technology bubble and stocks, the Bush (43) Administration would not criticize the housing bubble, and the Obama Administration will not criticize the artificially low interest rates.

Chapter Two

Globalization

As stated in the introduction, over 10 million American manufacturing jobs have been lost over the last 20 years. This has resulted in a dramatic decline in wealth of the middle class of the United States. It has also resulted in the higher levels of unemployment which I believe are structural in nature.

I believe this trend of globalization has impacted all the advanced economies—the European Union, Japan, England, and the United States. This was one of the primary reasons that the recession which began in 2008 was so severe and was a primary reason for the housing bubble.

Globalization has changed everything. It is causing significantly slower growth in advanced economies and is a primary cause of the plight of the middle class in the U.S. and other advanced countries. It has resulted in higher unemployment in advanced countries and a decline in U.S. labor union representation in the private sector of the United States to 6%, the lowest in nearly a century.

This severely affected the "tradable" portion of the U.S. economy. In addition to manufacturing jobs being outsourced, the reduced stature of labor unions and employees in general, has led to a dramatic decline in the relative compensation of employees.

My sister says something has to be done to restore the middle class. When I say that the plight of the middle class results from globalization and outsourcing of jobs, she says "you can't put the tooth paste back in the tube. Once it's gone it's gone." She may be right, but we have got to find a way to stop pushing more toothpaste out of the tube.

President Obama spoke in his campaign for re-election about establishing a Department of Business in the Administration. While I would question the need for a new department, there certainly needs to be a change in thinking regarding business. We have to compete for businesses the way other countries do. Whether this is done in a new department or in the Commerce Department, the U.S. must realize that other countries are competing to have companies headquartered there with the jobs associated with them. The U.S. tax and regulatory structure often discourage businesses from locating in the U.S.

If globalization is the most important economic trend of the past 25 years, why is it not discussed more by politicians and economists? First, we need to recognize that most economists that appear in the media are political economists who represent one side or the other of the aisle. Moreover, economists are taught that free trade is good. From the work of Ricardo, two centuries ago, to the Smoot-Hawley tariffs that deepened the Great Depression, most economists distinctively state that free trade is good.

There have been some dramatic benefits to globalization and trade in the past 25 years. In China, it is estimated that over 5 million people have moved above the poverty level because of the benefits of globalist trade. But, it is hard to convince a 55-year-old textile worker in South Carolina, who lost his job when the textile mill moved to China, that there is any benefit from globalization.

NAFTA

I've always assumed that NAFTA—The North American Free Trade Agreement—was put in place in an attempt to encourage job creation and economic growth in northern Mexico. The border between the U.S. and Mexico separates the widest disparity of wealth of any border in the world. Under these conditions, the continued migration of people from Mexico to the U.S. is assured.

Mickey Kantor, the NAFTA czar under the Clinton Administration, stated at one point that four or five jobs were being created in the U.S. for every job that was being outsourced to Mexico. I have no idea where Mr. Kantor got this information and, unfortunately, neither did he. Kantor was evidently harkening back to the theories of Ricardo, who we discussed earlier in the book.

During the 1992 Presidential campaign, H. Ross Perot described NAFTA as being a "giant sucking sound" pulling jobs from the U.S. to Mexico.

One important feature of NAFTA was the rethinking of so many companies as to whether or not they should consider moving their company's manufacturing to a foreign country. Although companies were always supposed to do things that are in the best interest of shareholders, I believe that until NAFTA was created, there was less emphasis on the possibility of moving jobs to another country. Even though more jobs are outsourced to China than to Mexico, I still believe that NAFTA was an important demarcation in the thinking of many corporate executives.

I do not know why politicians and economists are so reluctant to point to what seems so obvious: the introduction of billions of new workers into the world's labor force following the 1989 fall of communism in the Soviet Union, the opening of Eastern Europe, and the growth of China into the second largest economy in the world, which is destined to be the most powerful economy in the world within the next five to ten years. Perhaps politicians in both parties want to avoid the subject because there are no easy solutions. We obviously cannot go back to when imports were such a small part of economic activity. However, if we do not recognize the impact from the increased trade in globalization, I believe it will be extremely difficult to find solutions. The GOP "solution" of reducing the size of government is unrealistic, as is the Democratic penchant for larger government.

U.S. Trade in Goods and Services
1960–2010, in billions of US $

The disparity between the wealthy and the poor in the middle class in the U.S. has gotten much more extreme.

Hedrick Smith, in his book, *Who Stole the American Dream?*, quotes an estimate by Robert Scott, an economist at the American Policy Institute, that in the past 20 years, 2.5 million American jobs have been lost to China. In contrast, he notes that economists such as Alan Greenspan, again citing the work of David Ricardo, believed that there is no net impact on jobs. They believe that jobs outsourced, such as in textiles, are replaced by new jobs, for example, in technology. Paul Samuelson, who was an economic advisor to Kennedy, at 89 years of age, entered the debates saying that the wage disparity between China and the U.S. simply overpowers the old rules as theorized by Ricardo. Further, he points to the indirect effect of globalized trade as causing a reduction in the compensation for American workers. Obviously,

I agree with Scott and Samuelson. I believe the dogmatic adherence to the Ricardo principles simply lack common sense and defy the evidence of the last ten years.

Most Americans think of Mexico as a lawless land where drug gangs battle for supremacy near our border and where thousands of Mexican citizens attempt to cross the border into the U.S. That is part of the story. However, Mexico has experienced dramatic growth since the NAFTA treaty was passed 20 years ago, with U.S.-Mexican trade having tripled in that period. In an article in the March/April 2013 edition of *Foreign Affairs*, Shannon O'Neil concludes that Mexico has made a transition from a commodity based economy to one based on manufacturing and services, outpacing even China and India in making this economic transition. While Mr. O'Neil's article emphasizes the mutual benefits of increased trade, I am convinced that the outsourcing of U.S. manufacturing jobs is a primary cause of the plight faced by the American middle class.

Economist's views on globalization

Virtually all economists favor free trade. For more than two centuries, classical economics has favored free trade—and with good reason. Barriers to trade are frequently politically expedient and do not produce the beneficial results that politicians claim. Thus, the economic community found itself advocating free trade.

In his modern day classic, *The World is Flat*, Thomas Freidman had to deal with the issue of whether or not in a globalized society some countries would benefit and others would not. Or better said, some countries would benefit more than others. In chapter 20 of his original book, the author summed up the views of economists as being "I sure hope Ricardo was right." This was the smallest chapter in the book but as years passed with each new edition, the argument became more nuanced, the chapter increased in length, and it ultimately led, I believe, to the writing of a subsequent book called *That Used To Be Us*. Friedman clearly had difficulty from the beginning in squaring the traditional or classical economic views with the realities of the ways of energetic young workers that he saw in India and China. So who is this guy Ricardo and what did he say about free trade?

David Ricardo was a contemporary with Adam Smith, the patron saint of free market economics. He was a very successful businessman and a Member of Parliament.

In addition to the bias favoring free trade from the classical economics school, we also had the case of Smoot-Hawley tariffs and their impact on the Great Depression. It has long been believed that Smoot-Hawley tariffs enacted by the U.S. caused the depression to be considerably worse and considerably longer than would have been the case otherwise.

But, while I agree that political attacks on free trade are usually self-serving and ultimately lose more for a country than it gains, this does not mean that the sudden introduction of hundreds of millions of workers into the global labor force will be without negative consequences for the countries which are economically more advanced. That is why I maintain that the economic problems of the European Union, the U.S., England and Japan are very similar. Globalization reduces the potential growth rate in the economies of the advanced countries. Further, it creates a structural problem with unemployment and reduces the pay of the labor force. In certain respects, globalization was responsible for the overstimulation of housing in several countries, and led to the deep 2008-2009 recession.

I should note that many economists share my views that globalization is more important in the economic slowdown of the advanced countries than is generally believed.

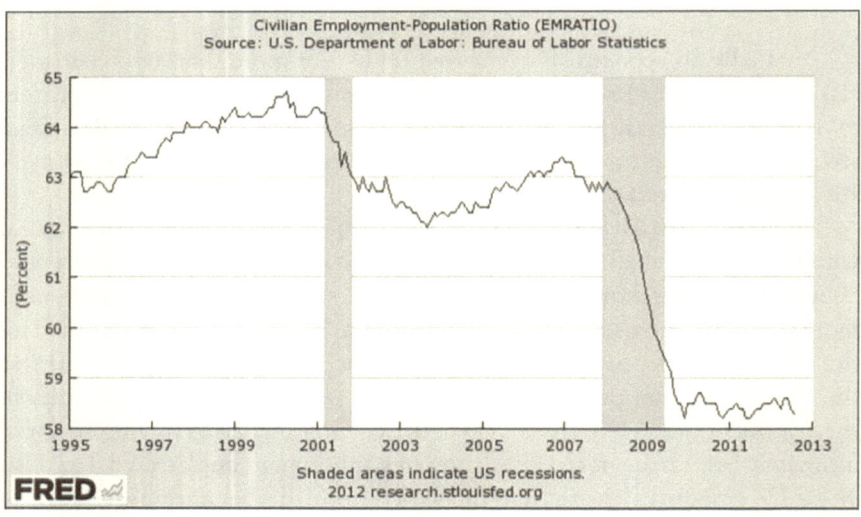

In his excellent and heartfelt work, *Who Stole the American Dream?*, author Hedrick Smith recites the views of many economists. Some, like Larry Lindsey, an economist with the Bush (43) Administration, simply say that the benefits of globalization are approximately equal to the negative impacts. From the cost of televisions and apparel, to the global search for dominance in the smartphone industry, there is no question that international competition has produced dramatic benefits. However, that does not mean that the benefits are equally distributed—at least not in the short term. Approximately 500-750 million people have been lifted above the poverty line in China alone. While China, in particular, has had extraordinary economic growth over the past 20 years, these benefits have not accrued to the more advanced countries. The belief that the outsourcing of manufacturing jobs would lead to an increase in more advanced jobs in the U.S. has simply not been borne out in practice.

More orthodox market fundamentalists, such as Alan Greenspan, dispute the idea that trade has caused job losses in the United States. Their view, as with British economist David Ricardo 200 years ago, is that free trade is good for both parties.

I vividly recall Fed Chairman Greenspan being questioned by the House Financial Committee and being asked what he would do if he were a textile worker in the Carolinas whose plant had moved to China. He responded that he would look for a job that emphasized something cerebral. I thought "you're a smug, elitist SOB." At least you could show some sympathy for workers who have lost jobs to outsourcing.

Economists such as Clyde Prestowitz disagrees and states that economists have been "invoking false doctrines that have systematically undermined American prosperity."

In the book cited before, *This Time is Different*, Ken Rogoff says that this line is often used to justify the overvaluation of particular stocks, real estate, commodities, etc. However, every cycle is different in some respects. And, one of the major differences since 1992 has been the impact of globalization generally. Democratic economists seem to be intent on stating that the problems are cyclical and not structural in nature. However, the structure has changed dramatically in the past 20 years. I suppose Democratic economists are concerned that if it is concluded that the problems in the economy are structural, there will be less emphasis on actions to improve conditions.

So what should we do?

So what should be done to reverse this trend or at least to moderate it? Certainly the idea of imposing tariffs on trade generally makes no sense. Just as the classical economic theories stated, there are indeed benefits from free trade. My sister says that we should deal with the consequences of free trade which has helped to produce the massive discrepancy between winners and losers in countries such as the United States.

I think that while the trend cannot be reversed, certain sub-trends are now occurring which at least will limit the negative impact of globalization, and will also recover some jobs in the U.S. First, there is greater awareness now of the need to emphasize manufacturing jobs in the U.S. This was evident in Obama's 2012 State of the Union address and his inaugural speech.

Second, there is also more appreciation for the disruption produced in the manufacturing of various products by having a portion of it outsourced. The more favorable cost of labor is frequently counterbalanced by transportation costs and the need to react rapidly to changing market conditions with a unified work force. Third, we simply asked some companies which outsource jobs to be more patriotic. A good example is Apple Inc., which will be producing Apple iMacs in the U.S. for the first time in more than a decade. In the concluding chapter I will recommend that this effort be enhanced. Whether the administration seeks to conduct this activity in a new Department of Business or in the Commerce Department, it is an essential element of any administration operating in the globalized world. One of the founders of Intel, Andy Grove, has stated that the U.S. is one of the worst countries in the world in which to operate, and that the U.S. does nothing to develop businesses whereas every foreign country would offer a package of benefits to Intel for locating in that country.

Some concluding thoughts

It is my belief that the current political and economic environment underestimates the impact of globalization on the U.S. and the other advanced countries. Politicians simply do not want to admit it because the solutions are quite difficult. The admission that a portion of the economic problem in the U.S. is structural in nature seems to some to take pressure off the government to intervene in an effort to stimulate the economy. And many economists, especially those aligned with one party or the other, who appear in the media most frequently tend to underplay the role of globalization in the slow economic growth and higher unemployment that is obviously a problem in the U.S., the European Union, England, and Japan. Recognition of the problem does not provide a solution, but I would maintain that any solution must start with recognition of the source of the problem.

Further, if I am correct in my belief that globalization is producing a structural impact on the U.S. economy that results in slower growth and higher unemployment, then the Federal Reserve's efforts to hold down interest rates until we have achieved a 6.5% unemployment level, will require a long period of purchasing Treasury bonds. Again this is producing an environment in which savers are unfairly penalized and the fiscal policies of the federal government are not penalized for the extraordinary deficits now being run. This latter point is important. Critics of the current level of deficit spending are not taken very seriously when they have ethical problems associated with leaving our current debt-producing ways to be resolved by future generations. While this argument is indeed correct, market conditions are masking the problem. The Federal Reserve must take some responsibility in allowing the federal government to operate with these excessive deficits, apparently without penalty, based on the current level of interest rates. While Mr. Bernanke does periodically remind Congress of their responsibility to move the budget toward a more balanced approach, the actions of the Federal Reserve speak louder than their words.

TV commentators can point to the low levels of interest rates and the strong U.S. dollar as demonstrating that the critics of the budget deficit are simply wrong in their beliefs that negative consequences will arise from the deficit. If the U.S. debt reaches 80% of GDP, as the current administration budget indicates, and when interest rates normalize to 5% then the interest on the debt would amount to 4% of GDP. This is roughly twice the cost of the debt in recent decades, and complicates the ability to balance the federal budget. Keep in mind that total government expenditures have averaged 19-20% of GDP in recent years, and the increased cost of interest on the debt, plus the increased cost of health care will make balancing the budget at 20% of GDP almost impossible.

This indeed makes the Federal Reserve part of the problem. Again, the Federal Reserve is masking the problems that the debt is causing by keeping interest rates artificially low. The Fed is essentially not allowing market signals (higher interest rates) to function.

Chapter Three

Asset Bubbles

When I was studying economics at William and Mary in the late 1960s, asset bubbles were thought to be either a quaint historical item, such as the tulip bulb mania in Holland in the 1500's, or something too awful to be repeated, such as the stock market bubble of 1920s and the ultimate crash in 1929. The subsequent depression, which lasted a decade and produced 25% employment, was far worse than anything experienced in any economic setback in U.S. history.

This period also produced an economist named John Maynard Keynes. Keynes rewrote the study of economics. Among other things, he asserted that federal government should operate at deficits when times were tough in order to stimulate the economy and spur economic growth. Paul Samuelson, the Dean of the Keynesian economist in the 1960s, wrote an academic essay stating that the fiscal budget should never be balanced. It should operate at a deficit in weak periods and at a surplus in stronger periods. Mr. Samuelson believed at the time that we could not only prevent future asset bubbles, but we could actually eliminate or greatly alleviate the business cycle. But, just as Plato found that there were no philosopher kings to sit upon the throne, Samuelson found that there were no economists/presidents to rule the U.S. Indeed, beginning in 1968 we had four recessions in 14 years, and we have had 40 years of some of the most powerful bubbles in economic history.

Economic bubbles do not appear in a vacuum; there is always some event or some trend of events which cause the bubble. The first bubble of note in the post-World War II period was the commodity bubble of the late 1970s. This was caused by the two OPEC-induced oil shocks and the systemic inflation which it induced. By the end of the 1970s, consumer prices increased by double digits on an annual basis as did salaries and some interest rates were over 20%. In this chapter we will look at Paul Volcker's heroic efforts to bring the runaway inflation under control.

From the commodities bubble and the high inflation period of the 1970s there were two echo bubbles which culminated near the end of the decade. As a result of the commodities bubble, and the "Eurodollar" market, huge loans were made in South America to produce everything from silver to nickel to copper to gold to platinum.

In the late 1990s we had the most clear cut bubble in recent history. Technological advances in personal computers, wireless communication, and in cell phones produced an equity bubble of historic proportions in the late 1990s.

And then we had the housing bubble; in many ways the most powerful bubble of them all and the most devastating. I'll describe this bubble in detail.

While this book is primarily about the bubbles in the U.S., this being the world's largest economy, whatever happens here impacts the rest of the world. However, there was one bubble of note that occurred in Japan in the late 1980s. This bubble was a combination of assets, real estate, housing, stocks, etc. and, consequently, it was the most ferocious and devastating bubble that has occurred in the last 40 years.

Have we learned our lesson? No says Ken Rogoff, co-author of the excellent book on the subject, *"This Time is Different,"* because bubbles are created by human nature. I will make the case that the next bubble is indeed currently building and it will be in the U.S. and international bond markets.

Echoes from the inflation period of the 1970s—South American loan bubble

The only asset, which I characterize as a bubble condition, which did not crash is the South American loans that were made late in the 1970s and the early 1980s. These loans were made primarily by the money center banks of the U.S. and their London operations.

This is a forgotten chapter of U.S. finance: the Eurodollar market in London in the late 1970s and early 1980s. The London offices of J.P. Morgan, Citibank, Chase Manhattan, Manufacturers Hanover, First Chicago, and other banks were receiving dollars primarily from Saudi Arabia and other OPEC countries, which were recycled as the U.S. purchased oil during the 1970s. Because of a strange twist in the banking regulations of the day these dollars had to remain in London. The banks, looking for loans to make with these dollars, concentrated their efforts on loans to South America. Loans were made to virtually every South American country in large quantity, to finance the mining of silver, gold, copper, nickel, etc.

For a while, everything went fine until the early 1980s when Paul Volcker led the U.S. into two recessions and was heading to a third, in order to break the back of the inflationary cycle, but Mexico was a problem. This left the countries of South America with huge debts for projects which were no longer economically justifiable because of the drastic decline of commodity prices. In South America those periods are known as the "lost decade," because the countries had to continue to make payments on loans for projects which were no longer economically viable. It was a concern at the time that if the countries could have banded together, as had OPEC, they could have demanded that the loans be written down, or they could have crashed the U.S. banking system.

Walter Wriston, the head of Citibank held an oft-stated theory that countries could not go bankrupt. In retrospect, I believe his theory was wrong, but it was the accepted theory of the day.

This problem festered throughout the Reagan years and was only addressed in 1989 by George H. W. Bush. By converting the loans to a series of Brady bonds, named for his Treasury Secretary, Nicholas Brady, the problem finally brought to a close. How close we came to a catastrophe we'll never know for sure. But, I feel that the vast holdings of South American debt on the balance sheets of the major banks of the U.S. had the potential to bring down the banking system.

As an aside, I was in charge of investments at the time for a regional bank headquartered in Roanoke, VA. We had major investments in Eurodollar CDs and Certificates of Deposit in major U.S. banks. However, the extent of the Latin American loan portfolio was unknown even to our credit advisors in New York. The head of a large Virginia ministry named Pat Robertson, for some unknown reason, believed that the Eurodollar market was going to collapse. Pat Robertson has a TV program called The 700 Club on which he predicts the occurrence of various things around the world. I do not know why he came to believe that the Eurodollar market was going to crash, but one of our board members was a financial supporter of Mr. Robertson, and he believed strongly that Pat Robertson was correct in his prediction of a collapse in the Euro market. He would call me from time to time, on Tuesday nights as I recall, to tell me that Pat Robertson would be talking about the Eurodollar market in his upcoming program. He felt so strongly about the potential demise of the Eurodollar market that he ended up resigning from our Board of Directors.

If a more credible spokesman had come to the same conclusion as Mr. Robertson, or if the general public had realized the extent of the loan portfolio to Latin American countries, which were for projects which were no longer viable, the outcome could have been very different.

Echoes from the high inflation period—the commercial property bubble

Savings and Loans Associations, S&Ls as they are called, took in deposits and made loans for residential mortgages. After the release of the movie, *"It's a Wonderful Life"* with Jimmy Stewart, they were perceived to be the good guys of the financial industry in the U.S. However, their portfolio of 30 year fixed rate mortgages, which was funded with much shorter terms CDs—Certificates of Deposit—obviously caused earnings problems in the high inflation period of the 1970s. This problem also festered throughout the Reagan years and only came to light in 1991-1992 in a brief recession. S&Ls were permitted to make real estate loans, either commercial or residential, but most concentrated on residential loans. However, in an attempt to get out of the negative interests rates environment (short rates above long rates), which result in a negative net interest margin environment, many S&Ls took on more risky commercial real estate loans. Throughout the 1980s, S&Ls were encouraged to go into commercial real estate by their regulators. When an S&L was examined, and the yield on a residential mortgage portfolio was less than the S&L's cost of funds, the regulators criticized them for not making more commercial real estate loans where the interest rate was a variable rate usually based on the prime interest rate. As an example, the largest S&L in Roanoke, VA was taken over by an investment group who used their deposits to invest in commercial real estate. They funneled the deposits into projects which they had a financial interest in, even though that was prohibited by regulation. This S&L went bankrupt.

A friend of mine showed me the financials of an S&L in a small town about 50 miles from Roanoke with syndicated loans from Arizona and Colorado. His father was a member of the Board of Directors of the institution, and he asked me what could be done. I told him unfortunately there was no hope. It was just a matter of time before the S&L would have to declare bankruptcy.

The only S&L that survived in Roanoke was run by a friend of a friend of mine. He said if he had done what the regulators encouraged him to do, his institution would have gone bankrupt as well. Fortunately, the S&L was allowed to recapitalize to survive.

It is amazing to see some of these things in retrospect.

The technology bubble

I distinctly recall a conversation with my friend, Peter, who headed up a local investment firm in the 1990s. We were chatting over a couple or three beers after a tennis match. He was lamenting the fact that technology stocks were dramatically over valued. I kidded him that he just didn't understand the new paradigms of the new era in investing. Peter was having none of it. Obviously he was having some difficult discussions with clients who wondered why their investment accounts were not growing at 25% a year as was the NASDAQ Index. He said, "We are not going to go this route at our firm. Our firm will be better off and our clients will be better off staying away from these overvalued assets. This thing is not going to end nicely."

This vividly illustrates how people can get caught up in this type of mania; some months later Peter and I were playing tennis with a friend who is also in investment management. Our friend, over a couple of beers after another tennis match, said that he had lost over a million dollars in the first quarter of 2000. But, he said that was just on paper. No, said Peter calmly, those are real losses.

I recall these instances to point out how two investment professionals, two very smart investment professionals, can view the financial market so differently. Obviously, in retrospect, my friend Peter was exactly right in his assessment of the situation while our mutual friend was completely wrong in his assessment. It is extremely difficult to recognize a real bubble when it is occurring.

Chapter Four

Home Ownership in the U.S. and the Housing Bubble

American's attitude toward housing was perhaps best depicted in the movie, *It's A Wonderful Life* starring Jimmy Stewart. As the president of a small town savings and loan association he did battle with the greedy, Dickensesque banker. Housing finance with 30-year fixed rate mortgages made the dream of an affordable house come true for millions of Americans during the 1950s and 1960s.

After World War II, the U.S. experienced a tremendous housing boom. These homes were financed by 30-year fixed rate mortgages at modest interest rates, with a 10 or 20 percent down payment. A provision of the "GI Bill" guaranteed many of these loans. This guarantee was usually unnecessary because the home prices continued to go up. Mortgage foreclosures were extremely rare during the 1950s and 1960s, when mortgage loans were usually the safest loans a bank could make.

Levittown-type communities sprang up across the country. And this too was a major factor in preventing the return to a recession or depression-type condition after World War II, which many had prophesized.

Mortgage financing was usually arranged by local, mutually owned Savings and Loan associations. Mutual ownership was an important aspect of these associations; not having to produce a profit for shareholders allowed these S&Ls to operate with only a small margin between the rate paid on customer savings and the rate charged for home mortgages. Further, S&Ls took on a benevolent community orientation again as depicted in Jimmy Stewart's S&L in *It's a Wonderful Life*.

The high inflation 1970s

As noted in the previous chapter, the high inflation of the 1970s changed everything. By the end of the 1970s, most S&Ls were operating with a negative interest rate margin. That is, they were paying more for the customer's deposits than mortgage loans were yielding, because the mortgage loans had such long maturities. If there had been a realization that Paul Volcker would be able to engineer a crusade to drive down inflation, they could have stuck to their plan, allowing their cost of funds to decline, and continue to operate as before. However, the federal S&L regulators became concerned and began to emphasize the need to increase the proportion to variable rate loans in the S&L's portfolio, at just the wrong time.

While their charters restricted lending them to real estate related lending, there was no provision that restricted commercial real estate lending.

In the 1980s, cities across the country experienced a building boom financed in large part by the S&Ls. Loans were frequently made on a long term mortgage amortization schedule with a three—to five-year call (refinancing). These so-called "mini-perms" were made on the assumption that real estate prices would continue to increase as they had during the 1970s.

However, when the Federal Reserve, under the leadership of Paul Volcker, dramatically reduced the growth of the money supply, inflation and interest rates began to ebb. As inflation declined so did the value of real assets. As the prices of oil, gold, and other commodities declined, so did the price of commercial real estate. The problem festered through the Reagan years, and when it finally crashed in 1990-92 it produced an economic recession which ultimately led to the ouster of President Bush (41) and the election of Bill Clinton.

So called COLT loans, those originated in Colorado, Oklahoma, Louisiana, and Texas, were frequently brokered to small S&Ls around the country. These loans were frequently sold by firms in Little Rock and Memphis, as well as Wall Street. When the bubble burst in the early 1990s, this wiped out many of the Savings & Loans in the United States.

In fairness to the Bush (43) Administration, it should be noted that there are a lot of reasons to be positive regarding housing. Data reveals that homeowners have more positive scores on everything from prospects for committing a crime, to the grades of their kids, and the probability that their kids will go to college. While some of these results are coincidental, when they are taken together, they are strong reasons to be positive regarding home ownership.

Further, for most people, their home is their largest and best investment.

Securitization to the rescue

Securitization is the process of creating a security backed by a pool of loans with similar characteristics. These securities could be backed by auto loans, credit card receivables, student loans, etc. But, by far, the largest group of loan backed securities are those backed by 30-year fixed rate home mortgages.

These mortgages have a feature which makes them very attractive to the borrower, but cause the greatest difficulty in the securitization process. That is, these mortgages can be repaid at any time without penalty. So if interest rates remain the same or go higher, the expected life of the home loan is much longer than if interest rates decline. This lengthening is due to fewer mortgage prepayments. This feature means that mortgage backed securities are sold based on a projected average life instead of the stated maturity date.

Wall Street firms began to create mortgage backed securities in the 1980s as S&Ls were unable to make the traditional type of mortgage. This was because of interest rate variability and its effect on S&L's cost of funds. However, the mortgage backed security market did not really take off until the Federal National Mortgage Association (Fannie Mae) and the Federal Home Loan Mortgage Corporation (Freddie Mac) began to guarantee the mortgages which were backing the securities created. These mortgage backed securities were later subdivided into layers, called tranches, with short average life securities receive the initial cash flow payments of principle pay down. The intermediate securities tranches received the second level of cash flows, and the longer securities receiving the final payments. Banks took the shorter terms securities into their portfolios. Life insurance companies and pension funds were the investors taking the longest securities. These securities were rated AAA because of the guarantee of Fannie Mae and Freddie Mac (quasi government agencies) and were an immediate hit.

Fannie Mae and Freddie Mac had once been agencies of the federal government, but their status was changed in the mid-1980s. These companies issued stock which was owned by the public and were now referred to as government sponsored enterprises or GSEs. This produced a conflict of interest almost immediately, but more on that later.

The average life of home mortgage loans is projected to be about 12 years with no change in interest rates. This shortened projected life is because most mortgages are not held to their 30-year term, but are paid off early because the home owner sells the house or prepays the mortgage for other reasons.

Fannie Mac and Freddie Mac securities were so popular that by 1992 they could be sold to investors at approximately 1¼% over the 10-year Treasury. Mortgages remained at approximately 1½% over the 10-year Treasury, and

Wall Street took a cut of about ¼% for creating the mortgage, thus a net sales rate of 1¼%. These new securities revolutionized the mortgage market.

In the early '90s I spoke with the chief economist of Fannie Mae at a meeting in Charlotte. He said Fannie Mae and Freddie Mac were both genuinely surprised at the popularity of the new securities. In fact, the 1¼% spreads were smaller versus 10-year Treasuries than when S&Ls originated the mortgages in the 1960s and 1970s. Thus, home ownership became even more affordable with the advent of securitization.

Also of note in the 1980s was the return to normalcy of interest rates following the high inflationary period in the late 1970s. With Paul Volcker's persistence, inflation was dramatically reduced and interest rates followed suit. Thus, by the end of the 1980s, the housing market was booming with the pent up demand from the 1970s.

The housing bubble grows

Through the 1990s, the housing market performed well. The mortgage market was well-funded, with 30-year fixed rate mortgages guaranteed by Fannie Mae and Freddie Mac providing the bulk of mortgage funding, at very reasonable interest rates.

There was some concern that Fannie and Freddie were becoming too political. This was especially true at Fannie Mae under the high profile leadership of Franklin Raines. Raines interrupted his lucrative tenure at Fannie Mae to head the Office of Management and Budget under President Clinton. There were also concerns about the compensation arrangement at Fannie Mae and Freddie Mac. The unusual structure of partial public ownership of these two huge companies, and the backing of the Federal government for financing, created many conflicts.

In late 1999, near the end of his term, President Clinton expanded the requirement under the Community Investment Act, which mandated that Fannie and Freddie provide more mortgage financing in relatively poorer areas in the U.S. This little noticed modification, according to some observers, was the single most important event leading up to the subprime mortgage crisis in 2007-2008.

Summary: The technology bubble burst shortly after Bush (43) was elected president in 2000. He enacted a series of tax cuts following Reagan, who believed that deficits were okay if caused by tax reductions. In retrospect, I believe the tax reductions squandered the first true surplus in modern times which occurred during the last two years of the Clinton presidency. The 9/11 tragedy changed everything. In the economy, the fairly mild recession in 2000 caused by the bursting of the technology bubble became more entrenched.

Preparations to go to war increased the deficit which had been brought about by the tax cuts. The Federal Reserve decreased interest rates even further to 2%. For a long period of time the low interest rate environment gave a lift to the housing sector, as is usually the case.

The growth in the housing sector was cheered on by the Bush (43) Administration, which viewed the sector as a spark to get the economy moving again. Federal Reserve Chairman Greenspan announced a plan to hold down interest rates for a prolonged period of time. Starting in 2004, the overnight federal funds rate would be increased by ¼% per quarter for two years.

On most of the economic trends that I have discussed, Roanoke, Virginia was a good place to watch trends unfold. As noted in the last chapter, for example, the technology sector-led stock market bubble affected people in Roanoke just as it affected people across the country. However, the housing bubble was not very pronounced in this part of the country. We could see announcements in the *Wall Street Journal* that condominium projects in Las Vegas and southern California were completely sold out before construction was completed, but nothing on that scale was happening here. On a national basis, GDP data made it clear how important the housing boom was with more than 50% of GDP growth coming from housing or housing related activities in 2004 and 2005. Federal Reserve Chairman Greenspan stated repeatedly that while housing prices were "frothy" in certain areas of the country, overall home prices were "well contained." The Bush (43) Administration cheered on the housing boom as part of the "ownership society." They hoped to include a revamped social security system as part of the ownership society, as stock prices advanced.

It should be noted that the housing boom affected other countries as well. In the European Union, similar economic conditions prevailed as in the U.S. Interest rates were low and there was little to ignite their economic recovery. Consequently, housing booms occurred in Ireland, England, and to a larger extent, in Spain. The Spanish economy, having the greatest housing bubble, has also had the hardest fall. Unemployment is currently 25% in Spain and the prospect for economic growth in the foreseeable future is low.

As described in chapter two, virtually all advanced economies in the European Union, the U.S., and Japan have outsourced jobs and are importing more manufactured goods from China. Housing is one of the few economic sectors where employment is created almost totally in-country. But when the housing boom ends, there is little to get the economy moving forward.

Wall Street has never been satisfied at splitting the bounty of the mortgage securitization process with Fannie Mae and Freddie Mac. And, with the housing boom they created a new type of home mortgage which could be marketed directly to borrowers, bypassing Fannie Mae and Freddie Mac. These mortgages were set at a variable rate with a very low initial fixed rate, usually lasting for the first two years of the mortgage. Since many people thought that home prices would always go up, it made sense to buy the largest home that you could. This is what the teaser rate period was designed to do.

For the most part, Wall Street firms did not directly market these new mortgages, but rather acquired them from mortgage companies. Among the companies operating on a national basis were companies such as Washington Mutual Savings, or WaMu, and Country Wide Mortgage. Other large players included companies such as IndyMac and GMAC. I received solicitations by mail from all four companies which have since gone bankrupt or were taken over by other companies. I responded to three. Their sales pitches went something like this: if your current mortgage rate is 5%, during the two year teaser period you could save $200 dollars per month. On a standard loan this would amount to a savings of almost $5,000 dollars during the two year period. So what happens at the end of the two year period? Their response was something like this: "our economics team projects that interest rates will decline and you'll be able to refinance at the end of two years at a fixed rate which will be as low or lower than the current teaser rate." Never mind that no such projection existed and the companies had no economic team.

I do not know why anyone would fall for this type of sales pitch. But, I suppose that is why a fairly large percent of victims were relatively financially undereducated. Others, it seems, were just caught up in the frenzy, and this mortgage product allowed them to buy a larger home.

Among the other fraudulent practices were falsifying documents relating to income and debt levels.

Prior to this period, subprime mortgages were a small corner of the mortgage business. It involved, for example, homes on a private road with no maintenance agreement, or a borrower that had an insufficient income stream, but had assets which could justify the mortgage. But as the housing frenzy grew, more and more mortgages were made on a subprime basis.

As the mortgage market got further and further extended, Fannie Mae and Freddie Mac reached a decision point: it would have to decrease the quality of their mortgages or get shut out of the market. Needless to say, their decision was to decrease mortgage quality. Moreover, they inaccurately disclosed the quality of the mortgages for almost two years.

Special note should be written about the credit rating agencies: Moody's, Standard & Poor's, and Fitch. On most mortgage securities, two of the three were required to rate the security. This produced a competition among the three as to who could justify placing a coveted AAA rating on the security. Since the mortgage originator paid the fees, and the originator of the mortgage select the rating agency, they got the security rating they wanted (AAA) and paid the fees, which compounded the problem. All three had computer models to assess the quality of the mortgages. However, all three assumed that home prices would not decline. There is no question in my mind that the ratings agencies were complicit in the fraudulent practices of the era. The question is whether or not they could be proven guilty. The federal government has a belated case against Standard & Poor's, and we will await the outcome, probably for several years.

The other characters in this tragedy include home appraisers, real estate agents, closing attorneys, etc. A frenzy of this magnitude requires a lot of supporting cast members.

And let's not forget the home purchaser. While many were victims of fraudulent sales practices, many others were not.

I retired from a local insurance company in August of 2008. My last conversation was with Steve Hilbish, who is going to take over many of my responsibilities. As I was leaving the office, Steve yelled and said "hey, what do you think is going to happen to Lehman Brothers?" I said confidently they (the federal government) will arrange a bail out similar to what they did with Bear Stearns. That was my last conversation at work. Of course they did not bail out Lehman. And, so the first weekend of my retirement, Lehman went under. And, of course, this threatened the entire financial system.

Some concluding comments

As noted previously, controlling asset bubbles is the implied responsibility of the Federal Reserve. This dual set of responsibilities of maximum employment and price stability carries with it the implication that the Federal Reserve must attempt to smooth out the business cycle as much as possible. However, Alan Greenspan's statement that the Federal Reserve's responsibility was merely to step in when bubbles burst is just not rationale.

Further, administrations in power cannot be the primary line of defense to protect against bubbles. The Clinton Administration welcomed the technology boom which led to a severe decline in stock prices in the ensuing recession. The Bush (43) Administration was ecstatic about the economic growth produced in the housing boom. And the Obama Administration is certainly pleased with the current artificial low interest rates.

And again, Wall Street's self-regulation is simply not rational. One of my favorite mutual fund managers, now retired, Jean-Marie Eveillard, says that on good days he considers the Wall Street machine to be the greatest sales force promotion that the world has ever seen. And on bad days, he thinks of it as a den of thieves. Morality and ethical behavior is simply contradictory to Wall Street's emphasis on profit maximization at both the personal and the corporate level.

But, greed is not attributable only to Wall Street in this saga. Real estate agents, appraisers, and closing attorneys are all part of the chain that created the housing bubble. And, let's not forget the home buyer. They are always portrayed as being victims of predatory lending, and this is true in many cases. But, many purchasers were out to make a fast buck as well flipping houses.

And a special note for the mortgage originators. The three that I spoke with were the sleaziest of salesmen, who would tell you anything to get you to do business with them. In many cases, pushing variable rate mortgages with a one—or two-year period of low interest rates, referred to as a teaser rate, was unethical. Many, if not most of these companies, no longer exist. They were either taken over by other companies or went out of business.

But, I have been surprised recently to have received a number of solicitations to refinance my existing mortgage. My mortgage is a VA loan, which I refinanced at $3\frac{1}{4}\%$ for 30 years on a fixed rate basis. So the companies that are contacting me are looking at my prior mortgage which was at $4\frac{1}{4}\%$. I received solicitations from companies with state charters in New Jersey. I would have thought with the mammoth, comprehensive, Dodd-Frank legislation, this type of solicitation would have been forbidden. After all, home financing is the largest financial transaction that most people make. I have contacted the Better Business Bureau, but I am not confident that any of these fraudulent, or at least misleading practices, will be stopped.

How did the folks on Wall Street explain what had occurred? Chuck Prince, the CEO of Citibank, said "as long as the music's playing, you've got to keep dancing." Robert Rubin, Chairman of the Executive Committee at Citibank, said that "even Greenspan didn't know how bad it was." And Alan Greenspan, Chairman of the Federal Reserve, said later before a Congressional committee that he had a "glitch in his model."

In fact, practically no one knew the extent of the problem. Very few, including Sid Bass of Texas and John Paulson in New York, bet that the housing bubble would burst so dramatically. But, I believe even they were surprised at the extent of the problem.

Greenspan once bragged that he had a hundred Ph.D. economists working for him at the Federal Reserve. Apparently no one was assigned to watch the mortgage market, which is by far the largest loan market in the United States. Many very good books have been written on the subject. These include personal accounts by both, Henry (Hank) Paulson, Secretary of the Treasury, and Ben Bernanke, head of the Federal Reserve. While these books explain in detail what occurred after the bubble burst, they do not explain how a problem of this magnitude could have gone undetected. Among the major players who apparently knew how bad things had gotten were J. P. Morgan and Goldman Sachs. Among the major bank casualties who clearly did not know the extent of the problems was Wachovia, which was forced into an acquisition by Wells Fargo. At Bank of America, their cross-town rival in Charlotte, NC, the acquisition of Countrywide Mortgage and Merrill Lynch crippled the bank.

One minor casualty was the insurance company where I worked. While we did not hold any of the subprime mortgage securities, our direct investment in Fannie Mae and Freddie Mac preferred stock helped to force a state-assisted acquisition by a Texas company.

As transcripts of the Federal Reserve deliberations in 2007 are made public, it is clear that the Federal Reserve did not realize the extent of the problems. Even though Alan Greenspan had retired as Chairman of the Federal Reserve, his view that home prices and mortgages were well-contained have prevailed. Apparently, the Treasury Department was in the same position.

However, while the major players clearly underestimated the extent of the problem, once Lehman Brothers failed, they were innovative and impressive. The Troubled Asset Relief Program, or TARP, that was designed to acquire assets from banks and other financial institutions was ditched and replaced with direct capital infusions into the banks. This enabled all the large banks in the country to continue to operate. While it is fashionable to criticize the TARP program as an undeserved bailout of Wall Street, damage to the economy of another major bank failure would have been devastating. And, because the TARP funds were directly injected into the banks there were funds remaining from the TARP program to bail out General Motors and Chrysler.

Greenspan's contribution

Chairman Greenspan, of the Federal Reserve, greatly influenced bubbles in general and the housing bubble in particular. As previously noted, he not only kept interest rates very low for a very long period of time creating an environment for the housing bubble to occur, but he also favored a self-regulation "scheme" whereby banks would regulate themselves. This probably kept the Federal Reserve from realizing the deteriorating quality of mortgage lines. He used his bully pulpit not to criticize the quality of mortgages being booked, but rather to emphasize that the bubble in housing would not occur. He stated repeatedly that the housing bubble was "well contained." I have no idea where he got this term from or what he meant, but he used it repeatedly. Looking back, it is hard to believe that he had so much power, so much influence on the thinking of everyone at that point in time. Even Robert Rubin, as he was leaving his palatial office at Citibank, said that when asked how he kept from knowing about the housing bubble he said even Greenspan did not know.

But, Greenspan's biggest contribution to bubbles in general, and the housing bubble in particular, was his theory that the Federal Reserve could not predict or intervene in the case of a bubble, but rather was relegated to the duty of cleaning up afterwards. This theory probably came from the criticism that he received in Congress for questioning the dot com bubble in December of 1996 when he posed the question of how one would know when "irrational exuberance" had caused stock prices to go beyond their underlying value. It is hard to believe that the bubble continued to grow for three full years after his questioning and he was criticized by Congress on several occasions for even posing the question.

Greenspan is supposedly coming out with a book in October of this year (2013) which will update his views on the world and correct the "glitch" in his model as he described it to the Congressional committee. Among the things that he is supposed to discuss is human nature. I assume that means he will attribute the bubbles to human nature, as did Ken Rogoff in his excellent book on the subject, and explain the "glitch" in his model by failing to recognize the weakness and fallacy of human nature in the process of economics.

Chapter Five

The Problem with Republicans

This book is not about gun control, nor abortion, nor gay rights, but rather about the financial and economic trends which we are currently experiencing and are likely to experience in the future.

The Deification of Ronald Reagan

In 1993, a friend of mine named John Francis asked if I'd been active in the Republican Party. He knew that I liked George Bush the first and thought I might have attended some Republican functions. When I told him that I had not, he said "You're missing something important. The Republican Party is making a god of Ronald Reagan." "I certainly liked Ronald Reagan," he continued, "but I'm amazed at some of the things they are coming up with."

And, of course, he was exactly right. The deification of Ronald Reagan remains one of the most important events in recent history of the Republican Party.

One particular aspect of the revisionist's history of Ronald Reagan that remains problematic today is that reducing taxes produced the economic growth of the 1980s and the resulting decline in unemployment. While the tax cuts probably had some positive impact on economic growth, it is important to recall that behind inflation and high interest rates during the 1970s greatly reduced economic activity. The Republican revisionist who rewrote the history of the period gave Paul Volcker no credit for his gallant efforts to bring inflation under control. This was perhaps because he was a Democrat appointed by Jimmy Carter or perhaps it was just to give Ronald Reagan credit for the entire Reagan tax cut credit that increased economic activity and reduction in unemployment.

I had a chance to meet Paul Volcker in 1980 when inflation was at double digits and interest rates were even higher. I did not sit at the head table where Paul Volcker was sitting, but I arranged to have the back of my chair next to the back of his chair so that I could overhear the conversation. He basically said that inflation was so entrenched that it had to be attacked. He realized fully that in order to deter inflation, a recession would eventually ensue. But, he stated with conviction that even though the Federal Reserve would have to temporally forgo their mandate to reduce unemployment, it was essential that they concentrate on bringing inflation under control. The resulting increase in interest rates produced a sharper recession in 1982. However, as inflation declined, the Fed gradually reduced interest rates and the economy began to recover. I recall that Mr. Volcker became quite animated after two or three glasses of wine that evening and emphasized inflation must be brought under control. In the early 1980s, Volcker engineered two recessions and was going to cause a third, but Mexico got in the way. This was the primary reason that we experienced a boom in economic activity in the 1980s. This is also why the tax cuts engineered by Bush (43) had so little impact on economic growth. Cutting taxes from 40% to 35% had little impact on the pace of economic activity.

Yet, many Republicans attribute the economic boom of the 1980s entirely to the tax cuts. Most Republicans appear to believe, without thinking, that lower tax rates produce more jobs and economic growth. Others believe that the lower level of tax revenue will make it more difficult for the Democrats to increase spending. Still others realize that the majority of Americans want to pay lower taxes, as shown in the survey data discussed in the introductory chapter.

Immigration

In 1992, a friend of mine and I were on a driving trip through the Midwest. One Sunday afternoon we were drinking Budweisers at a tavern in Dodge City just off Main Street. The owner of the tavern, who was also the local postmaster, was tending bar that afternoon because his regular bartender had called in sick. There was a separate section of the tavern with a couple of pool tables and pinball machines. There were about a dozen Mexicans in the room who were obviously enjoying their day off.

I said to the owner of the tavern that I was surprised to see the Mexicans in southern Kansas. He responded "who do you think works in these packing houses in the Midwest? If it wasn't for the Mexicans, every packing house in the Midwest would have gone out of business a long time ago."

This comment is the same one I have heard from farm owners in the Sacramento valley in California and owners of apple orchards in southwestern Virginia; "if it wasn't for the Mexicans we would go out of business."

So how did these Mexicans get here? A couple of years after my conversation with the bartender in Dodge City, Kansas, I was in Tucson, Arizona. I went down to the Mexican border town of Nogales. I drove down to the border, parked my car on the U.S. side of the border and walked across. This was prior to the drug smuggling days and everything was quiet and peaceful. In fact, the first thing that I saw when crossing the border was not the taverns, but large, modern looking White's Drug Store. I was told that these drug stores specialized in cancer treatment which were experimental and were not available in the U.S. I walked past the drugstores and sat on the verandah of a Mexican restaurant/bar.

A couple of hours later back on the U.S. side in the border town of Douglas, I struck up a conversation with a local guy and recalled the visit to Dodge City, Kansas a couple of years earlier. He told me that there was a bus which ran weekly from the outskirts of Douglas to the Midwest. The border crossing guides would arrange to have enough people cross the border by Wednesday or Thursday of each week to have a bus full going to work in the packing plants in Iowa, Kansas, etc.

I mention these two visits by way of pointing out how open illegal immigration was in the early—to mid-1990s. Neither political party made a big deal out of it. So for Republicans to have made illegal immigration such a major issue in the Republican debates and primaries leading up to the 2012 election was political hypocrisy of the highest order. Any chances of "self-deportation" ended decades ago.

Step back for a moment: the U.S./Mexican border is 1,933 miles long. It has the distinction of separating two populations with the widest wealth differential of any border in the world. In Mexico City they refer to the illegal immigration as migration.

Congressman Luis Gutierrez of Illinois, obviously a Latino, says further that more Mexicans have entered the country illegally by simply overstaying their work visas than by crossing the border.

Regardless, the number of people from Mexico and Central America who have entered the country illegally is far too great to consider deportation, self-deportation or otherwise. These illegal aliens or undocumented Latino workers, whichever you prefer, perform the most difficult and least rewarding jobs in the United States. Even in Roanoke, Virginia, Latinos provide a great deal of the unskilled labor needed for agriculture and construction. I will admit that most of the Latinos that I see work at local laundries, fast food places, and as helpers for plumbers, air conditioning people, etc. They work hard and are almost invariably pleasant.

The dilemma is simple: how do you make all of these people citizens of the United States, without rewarding them for breaking American laws. While the dilemma is simple, the solution is not. But, the idea of deporting millions of workers in the U.S. is obviously impractical.

The Republican Party needs to play a role in this debate. They need to do so in order to preserve the party, but also because it is the right thing to do and it is the only practical thing to do.

Ronald Reagan, you will note from the graph in chapter one, had a large deficit through his term in office. This is tantamount to a form of Keynesian spending.

But the GOP revisionists would have none of this. So far as the official Reagan record is concerned, it was solely a reduction of tax rates that brought about the prosperity of the 1980s.

The reduction in tax rates did have some positive impact, but so did the stimulus of a large deficit between government expenses throughout his entire presidency.

Moreover, I am convinced that the most important thing that occurred to reduce the unemployment rate was the return to normalcy in the interest rate structure as engineered by Paul Volcker.

While this book is primarily about financial and economic trends, I would like to close this chapter with a reference to the religious right. In years past the so-called religious right was a small fringe element of the Republican Party, but in recent years it has become more prominent. Religions by their very nature claim to be the ultimate truth. Politics, being aptly described as the art of compromise, makes it difficult to deal with a contingent of the party claiming to have the ultimate truth. This is obviously not to say that the evangelical movement should be excluded from the political process, however, I do believe some of the rigidity and failure to compromise among Republicans is partly attributable to the belief that positions are dogmatic Christian principles which cannot be compromised.

Chapter Six

The Problem with Democrats

The problem with Democrats—no surprise here—is spending. The nation's debt continues to increase by more than a trillion dollars a year in the fourth year of a recovery. A deficit of this magnitude can only continue because the Federal Reserve is holding interest rates at such a low level. With the number of people going into Medicare and Social Security, and with the increased interest costs of the national debt when interest rates do finally normalize, this will obviously be a long term proposition with no easy solution.

The Federal Reserve and the Obama Administration are obviously of the opinion that the economy will improve and will begin to grow at a pace that will more than offset this deficit increase. As I have stated before, I do not believe that in a globalized economy this will necessarily be the case, at least not in the long term.

The Health Care Problem

It is well known that the U.S. spends twice as much as other advanced countries on health care. Approximately 18% of our GDP is attributable to health care in one form or another, about half of that is federal, as compared to 9% on average for other advanced countries.

Paul Ryan had a "plan" that would have reduced the Medicare tab by giving retirees a "voucher" to spend on health care. Obviously, the effort was to try to get those on Medicare to have some skin in the game so they would be more mindful of the escalating health care costs and they would try to help reduce it by policing their activities.

The plan would only start 10 years from now when those currently 55 years of age were signing up for Medicare.

The President called a conference at George Washington University and had Paul Ryan sitting in the front row. My understanding is that Paul Ryan thought that he would take exceptions to certain parts of the plan but would agree with others, and they would have the opportunity to debate the issue. It's obvious, President Obama condemned the Ryan plan with the fervor of a hellfire and brimstone country preacher saying that is was un-American to even consider any reduction to Medicare. A few days later the Democratic Party began running the "throw granny off the cliff" political attack ads.

I did not think the Ryan proposal was practical because many seniors are simply not in a position to evaluate the merits of various medical expenses, and cannot negotiate with insurance companies over the cost of health coverage. However, I think Paul Ryan is to be credited with trying to come up with a plan which would reduce medical costs. Rather than doing what so many people in the Republican Party were doing—screaming about abortions or death panels–at least he was taking a thoughtful approach in reading the bill (which is no easy task) and trying to find some way to reduce costs.

That is why I believe that we have an impasse where the Republican Party is just saying that "we have a spending problem" without specifying health care as the major culprit. They are attempting to put pressure on the Obama Administration to come up with some mix of changes which would reduce the overall costs of Medicare.

Democratic commentators on TV seem to emphasize that the slow economic recovery is not a matter of structural changes in the economy, but rather is a cyclical problem. This problem is hard to get out of because the Bush (43) recession, as they refer to it, is so much deeper than expected. Many of these same commentators are now "experts" on the infrastructure needs of the country, just as they were "experts" on green energy during Mr. Obama's first term in office. Since green energy did not produce the number of jobs that they anticipated, they now have a new-found expertise in infrastructure spending.

Deficits do matter

Paul O'Neill, the first appointed Treasury Secretary under George W. Bush, describes in astonishment how Vice President Dick Cheney said "deficits don't matter. Reagan proved that." As discussed in the preceding chapter, Ronald Reagan did use deficit spending to stimulate economic growth far more than his current worshippers would have you believe. They give total credit for the economic growth during his term to the tax reductions. However, these deficits and the increased debt occurred during a time when the economy was growing rapidly and interest rates were coming down. Currently, neither of these trends exist.

Current liberal economist, Paul Krugman, the Nobel Laureate, also says that deficits don't matter, or more precisely, they don't matter now as much as the consequences of deficits which he assumes will generate distant economic growth. Mr. Krugman believes the "Bush (43) recession" was unusually deep by post-war standards and, consequently, will take more stimulus to recover. As noted in chapter one, I believe the outsourcing of 10 million American jobs during the past 30 years has made the prospect of rapid economic growth much more difficult than would have been the case in the past.

Whether rapid economic growth is used by right wing Republicans to justify balanced budgets or is used by left wing Democrats to justify deficits by increased spending, I do not believe either will be forthcoming. The Bush (43) tax cuts enacted in 2001 did not produce rapid economic growth and neither did the Obama stimulus of 2009.

Further, deficits do matter. To get some idea of the consequences of the current deficits, the Federal debt in the U.S. is approaching the annual Gross National Product ($15 trillion). If interest rates were to normalize at this historical 10-year Treasury at 5%, this would mean in simple terms that 5% of our GDP would go to pay interest on our debt. But, obviously, it would mean since we have historically run the federal government at about 20% of GDP, this level of interest rate payments would further reduce the prospect of longer term economic growth. And, coupled with the higher medical care and Medicaid payments and Social Security increases, it is difficult to see how we could come out of this without a sizeable increase in the Federal government to perhaps 25% or more of GDP.

Keynesianism has run amok

A woman with the Obama administration was discussing food stamps on NPR radio in early 2013. She said the multiplier effect of food stamps was 1.7 times, meaning that the economy benefitted tremendously from the food stamp program. Never mind that food stamps program (which is now called the SNAP program) has gone from 28 million people in 2008 to 48 million members at the end of 2012. She justified this as a way of growing the economy.

The number of people on Social Security (SS) disability has also increased dramatically. In 2008 there were fewer than 9 million people on SS disability. That has grown to almost 11 million currently. Nearly half of these disabled workers suffered from back problems or psychological problems. It is virtually impossible to disprove a person's claims to be suffering from back pain or psychological imbalance. Further, a cottage industry has grown up in the U.S. whereby lawyers advertise for clients with "disabilities." They have medical professionals on their staff to seal the deal through the Social Security maze. That is not to say that some of the people going on disability do not deserve it, but the system is obviously being gamed.

Medicaid enrollment has likewise increased from 45 million to 54.3 million. Again, this is not to say that the majority of these people are not entitled to Medicaid, but the increase is dramatic.

The number of Social Security disability recipients always increase when the economy is doing badly. And, obviously, food stamp enrollment increases as well. But to have the dramatic increases continue in the fifth year of a recession is unprecedented!

The Obama Administration and the Media

The media has been favorable toward President Obama from the very beginning. This bias was more pronounced in his first run for office than in 2012.

In early June 2012, I surveyed evening news reports regarding positive and negative articles on Romney v. Obama. Romney had just won the Republican nomination. It was his initial exposure to the national media as the Republican candidate for President. This was not intended to be a scientific survey; just notes from watching the national news programs. For three to four weeks I rated articles on the two candidates on ABC, CBS, NBC, CNN, and PBS. Of the 52 articles about either candidate, I rated 12 about Obama as being positive and zero negative. Conversely, Romney articles were one positive versus 10 negative. Again, this is not a scientific survey, but the bias is so pronounced that I do not believe anyone could consider the media to be neutral.

The one positive article on Mitt Romney was done by Judy Woodruff on PBS. She basically allowed the governor of Wisconsin to describe the positive traits of Mitt Romney with no interruption. I recall this vividly because it was so out of the ordinary at the time.

It should be kept in mind that this was a particularly bad time for Romney. He had defeated his Republican opponents by leaning far to the right and there were obvious questions about some contradictions with his earlier views as governor of Massachusetts. And I would point out that some of the coverage on Romney did get less negative later in the campaign, as his wife entered the picture.

My sister says that the media is not biased, but rather reports the facts which are negative for the Republicans and positive for the Democrats. Her theory is a somewhat modern day version of Harry Truman. When someone yelled "Give 'em hell Harry," Truman responded, "that he simply told the truth and the opposition thought it was hell."

The media has been supportive of President Obama through the first term and into the second. Recently, however, there has been some concern that they have gone too far. With the IRS scandal, the wire taps of AP reporters, the Benghazi attacks, and now the health care rollout, the media is concerned that they perhaps give the Obama folks too much of a pass.

Affordable Care Act and Its Aftermath

The Affordable Care Act is inaptly named. The U.S. already has the highest proportion of GDP devoted to health care, and adding millions of uninsured people to those that are insured will obviously increase the demand for health care. Health care already costs the U.S. 18% of its GDP—almost 50% more than any other nation in the world.

I will not attempt in this book to give my personal prescription for bringing health care costs under better control. But, with the U.S. government picking up a bigger and bigger portion of the cost of healthcare, it will obviously either crowd out the other possible programs or will add dramatically to the costs of government.

The term "Affordable Care Act" (ACA) is obviously used as a marketing tool to sell the concept to the American people. The Congressional Budget Office (CBO) did a study of the ten-year effects of the "Affordable Care Act" and concluded that the costs were covered by savings and by higher taxes. This ten-year period however, had tax increases occurring two to three years before the expenses occurred so it was flawed from the beginning. However, Debbie Wasserman Schultz, head of the Democratic Party, must have referred to the CBO study approximately 50 times in interviews as it was being debated in Congress. The Democrats obviously knew that this was not cost neutral. There is no way that you can add millions of people to health insurance without increasing the cost of healthcare. While technically she did not say anything incorrect, nor did the CBO do anything incorrect because everyone knew that the study was biased because of the time/cost mismatch of the revenue versus expenses. Nonetheless, the Democrats sold the "Affordable Care Act" to the American people on it being a program where revenues would cover the increased costs.

I would point out that this salesmanship pales in comparison to the selling of the Iraq war by the Bush (43) Administration, but nonetheless, I find it somewhat offensive that these sales techniques were used. Moreover, the ACA used another technique that is used by consulting companies: they find some popular element of a study that can be implemented quickly. In the case of the ACA this was the provision that students could remain on their parent's plan until the age of 26. This popular provision was implemented immediately to show the benefits of the program.

I believe one of the legacies of the Obama presidency will be the fundamental increase in the size of government from the 20% of GDP, which it has averaged since World War II, to probably 24-25% of GDP. This was caused in large part by the increase cost of government sponsored health care programs, primarily Medicare and Medicaid, and the increased interest costs of the federal debt. Further, I suspect that with the gridlock in Washington, taxes will not be increased sufficiently to pay for either program. As a result, we will end the period with an annual budget deficit of more than $500 billion even if the economy continues to grow modestly over the period.

Chapter Seven

Investing

The purpose of this chapter is to warn about the current investment environment: specifically, that the current level of interest rates are not sustainable and to suggest what investors should do to protect their investment position—whether 401K—from the inevitable decline in bond prices when interest rates do normalize. Further, I hope to persuade readers that they should take ownership of their investments—whether 401Ks or otherwise—and that investments should not be viewed as a chore, but as a positive, enjoyable experience. I'll then suggest some further readings to facilitate this process.

How to use a financial advisor
Stock mutual funds
Investing in stocks directly
Gold, silver and other commodities
Further readings and conclusions
Investing in equity mutual funds

Do not buy bonds

I have described the current Federal Reserve policy of holding down interest rates as a grand experiment. It has never been done before and the outcome is uncertain. No one knows if it ultimately produces inflation; it must come to an end at some point. And when that happens, interest rates will increase producing a decline in bond prices. A friend of mine, who is retiring from work in Atlanta, GA, is consolidating her retirement funds into a Roth IRA. I had advised her to do this because I believe that consolidated retirement funds can be managed better than having several 401Ks or IRAs.

She said she had a new financial adviser, one who works for the income and is not associated with any institution. I told her that I thought that this was a good idea. I went on to say that she should not buy any bonds. Her advisor on the other hand said that she should have 40 to 50% of her funds in bonds. She asked me what percent of my portfolio I had in bonds, and I said zero. Her advisor said that I must be joking because I should have at least 50% of my funds in bonds. I do not know whether she followed my or her advisor's advice regarding the bonds, but this is something that must worry Mr. Bernanke and the Federal Reserve. A 20-year Treasury bond is currently priced to yield 2¼%. Long term rates would go up to approximately 4½% if the Feds were not artificially holding down interest rates. This increase in yield would reduce the value of a 20-year bond by 18%. This is an example of what we are going to face when the Federal Reserve begins to allow interest rates to return to more normal levels.

I have a neighbor, who has remained in bonds, who he says that his bond funds are not doing great but they are doing okay and he just increased his holdings in the bond fund.

Buy houses and mortgage to the hilt

I have personally bought two houses recently and refinanced the third. The interest rate on 30—year fixed rate mortgages is between 3¼% and 3¾%. *This is a gift.* I do believe that housing prices have bottomed out in most parts of the United States. While it is difficult to get home mortgages, to the extent that you can do so, you are well advised to buy a bigger home, another home, or to refinance your existing home at current interest rates.

While I have philosophic questions about the Fed's actions regarding interest rates, it does not prevent me from taking advantage of the current level of interest rates.

Buy term insurance and invest the rest

During the 1990s, life insurance companies realized that they had to develop a product(s) in order to prevent their business from shrinking and going to mutual funds. So they devised a complicated menu of annuities which were indexed to the stock market or were based on other indices to form other variable annuities. These annuities are extremely expensive because of the sales charge that should almost always be avoided. While some of these plans are okay, the best rule is to simply buy term life insurance from a reputable company to cover your insurance needs and to invest the remainder into common stocks.

The Stock Market

This section is not for people who want to trade the markets, but rather it is for people who want to invest some money on their own outside their 401K. It is about buying a stock in a company with which you are familiar at a decent price and holding the stock as a long term investment.

The value of stocks or the stock market in general is measured by its relationship to earnings. This is called P/E ratio. The price to earnings (P/E) of the market in general is about 15 times. Currently the market's P/E is near the historical averages even though the stock market has hit all-time highs. A good place to find the P/E ratios of the various company stocks is to get the weekend *Wall Street Journal* which has a nice one page listing of the 1000 largest companies and their P/E ratios and other financial measures to research the stock of the company. Another important measurement of stocks is the dividend yield. For example, Duke Energy (DUK) trades at a very high 4.5% yield, but also equally high 23 P/E. Not surprisingly the high P/E is a result of the stock having increased in value because of the low interest rate environment.

Volatility of earnings is another method to value a stock. Ford Motor Company (F) trades at a 9 P/E because of perceived volatility of earnings. I will show the ticker symbols of the stocks that I mentioned. For example, Ford stock symbol is under the ticker symbol "F." Chevron stock, (CVX) the ticker symbol, also trades at a 9 P/E with 3% dividend on the belief that oil prices could decline causing a reduction in earnings. Target (TGT) trades at 15 times earning with a 2% yield, which is somewhat in line with the market. Eli Lilly (LLY) is trading at 15 earning with a 4% dividend yield. Kellogg (K) trades at a 19 P/E and a 3% dividend. A high yield on your cost basis is a measure of a good investment.

What I recommend that people do is to find a sector they enjoy or stocks that they have some affinity for, such as the company where they work.

Peter Lynch, the longtime head of Fidelity's Magellan Fund, a mutual stock fund, popularized the term "management by walking around" to describe the importance of looking at everyday stores and other companies when deciding what to invest in. For example, I own shares in Kroger (KR) where my wife shops and CVS where we buy our medicines. Target (TGT) is my daughter's favorite store for everyday items. A few years ago CVS went on a building spree with their stores being upgraded to stand alone stores; previously they were smaller stores usually attached to grocery stores. As

I watched this occurring in Roanoke, I realized it was part of a national program and I was convinced that with the population getting older and more drugs being sold, the drug store chain was going to flourish. I bought CVS at $15.00 a share. It is currently $50.00 a share and with a P/E of 17 and a 2% yield, I do not consider it to be overvalued.

Another example of stock selection was made when my daughter was a teenager. I would listen to she and her friends talking about what stores were hot—whether it was Abercrombie or American Eagle or whatever—and would invest in that particular store. The primary motive was to try to get my daughter interested in stock investing, but the secondary motive was to make some money. So we went from Abercrombie (ANF) to American Eagle (AEOS) to Hot Topics (HOTT). This worked out surprisingly well. My daughter did not get interested in the stock market, but the investment did prove out. This exposed me to a sector of the investment world that I would never have known otherwise. From Limited Too when she was 12-years-old to the teenage stores that I have mentioned above, to Coach (COH) and Michael Kors (KORS), I have followed her with investments.

For the most part however, I prefer to buy stock that I can hold for a very long period of time., I bought the stock about a year ago when DuPont (DE) went to $30 a share. It is now at $40, with a P/E of 4x.

So how do you get started investing? I check with my bank to see if they have an affiliate where you can trade by computer. I use Wells Fargo where the trades cost $29.00 for up to 1000 shares. I am aware that you can do the same thing at E-trade or Charles Schwab far less, but the transaction costs are inconsequential for what I am talking about. However, I would caution against the higher transaction costs if you go through a broker. I would question the broker and find out the costs; sometimes it is prohibitive. But, online purchases for under $30.00 are acceptable for the type of investment that I am referring to. One obvious thing that can be currently pursued is to pick stocks that have a good international presence. U.S. companies such as Caterpillar (CAT) with a 10 P/E and a 2.3% yield, or John Deere (DE) with an 11 P/E and a 2% yield are good examples. IBM (IBM) has a 14 P/E and a 2% yield.

Banks remain cheap. U.S. Bank Corp. (USB), for example, which had no problems in the recent financial crisis (2008-09), trades at a 12 P/E and a 2.5% yield. The Canadian banks are also inexpensive in today's market. Toronto Dominion (TD), which likewise did not have any problems in the financial crisis, trades at a 12 P/E and a 4% dividend yield.

Australian companies have also performed well during the recent period of financial turbulence with companies such as Westpac (WBK), a large banking group, paying a 4% dividend and trading at a reasonable P/E.

Likewise, Rio tinto (RIO) and BHP Billiton (BHP) trade at reasonable P/Es with yields of 4%, and are two of the largest mining operations in the world.

401Ks

The 401K has replaced the pension of most companies in the United States. The next section of the chapter deals with 401Ks, which, of course, are now the primary investment vehicle for retirement in the U.S. I will discuss the stock market in terms which I think everyone will understand. Everyone should maximize out their contribution to their tax-advantaged 401K. This is especially true if your company matches your contribution. This is easy tax free money.

I am amazed at how little most employees know about their 401Ks. Even very intelligent people working for very intelligent companies have deficiencies in their 401Ks or don't take the time to analyze their investments. While they say they are leaving the analysis to professionals, it is their money. Their retirement will depend in large part of the performance of the 401K.

Employees have the initial responsibility for the selection of the provider of the 401K. Instead they tend to decide on one asset allocation and never change until too late. Employees need to evaluate their holdings. This is especially true since the "safest" asset, i.e., Treasury Bonds, are now the most risky.

The stock market according to GARP

Growth stocks are more difficult to evaluate than value stocks. This is because they do not have the more predictable earning streams that larger value companies have. They also trade at premium prices and P/E's. The concept of growth at a reasonable price, or GARP, is a way to try to evaluate growth companies.

By creating a PEG ratio, or P/E divided by its growth rate, this gives the evaluation of growth stocks some analytical framework. For example, CVS, which I discussed earlier and which I bought as a value stock is now at an 18 P/E. In other words, it is now valued as a growth stock rather than as a value stock. This is success. However, I need a new way to evaluate the value CVS in terms of growth. The PEG ratio provides such a framework. If the P/E is 18 and the growth rate is 20 the PEG ratio is .9. Growth investors consider this to be a relatively undervalued growth stock; below 1.0 is a good ratio; 2.0 or above is a highly priced growth rate.

Chapter Eight

The Energy Revolution

The United States is in the midst of a tremendous energy boom. This boom has been brought about by the advancements and the technology related to "fracking." Fracking is a process which allows the production of natural gas and oil from shale and other tight formations. Fracking has been used for years, but the coupling of this process with horizontal drilling has produced amazing results.

In the past six years, U.S. production of petroleum and natural gas has jumped from 15 million barrels of oil (BOE) equivalence a day to 20 million BOE per day. Moreover, oil imports have fallen from 14 million barrels a day to below 8 million. This is the lowest level of oil imports in more than 25 years.

The impact on natural gas prices has been dramatic. U.S. natural gas is currently priced at $3.50 per million BTUs as compared to approximately $12.00 in Europe and $16.00 in Japan. The North American region should have a dramatic advantage versus Europe and Asia for years to come. It is projected that natural gas prices will remain between $3.00 and $5.00 per million BTU for the foreseeable future.

Oil is traded on an international market and is easily transported. The U.S. lacks this advantage in natural gas that can only be transported in a costly liquid form. And, yet, the price of oil in the U.S. is averaging 10% to 25% below the price in Europe and Asia. The International Energy Agency (IEA) predicts that the U.S. will surpass Russia and Saudi Arabia in oil production by 2020.

Prior to the attack on the World Trade Center and the Pentagon on 9/11/2001, there were only two reasons for American interest in the Middle East: oil and Israel. Were it not for oil, I do not believe the U.S. would have intervened in the first Gulf War to get Iraq out of Kuwait in 1990. Keep in mind that millions of people were killed in the African Congo and this hardly made the evening news.

I believe the same would have been true in the Middle East had it not been for oil and Israel. It is amazing how much of America's foreign policy is devoted to the Middle East. In the Presidential debate between Romney and President Obama, which dealt with foreign affairs, approximately three-fourths of the debate was about the Middle East. During the confirmation hearings of John Kerry for Secretary of State and Senator Chuck Hagel for Secretary of Defense, the questions and comments from the Senate Foreign Relations Committee were almost entirely on the Middle East.

I am thankful that the Bush (43) Administration made the decision to allow the various states to set their own policy regarding fracking. And I am also thankful that among the states benefiting in terms of jobs from the fracking were states such as Ohio and Pennsylvania. I suppose it shows my political cynicism, but I believe the Obama Administration would have been much more negative in their response to fracking if it had been entirely red states such as Texas and Oklahoma. But the fact that so many jobs were created in high unemployment areas in western Pennsylvania and eastern Ohio resulted in the Obama folks not allowing the EPA to interfere.

Natural Gas

On a BTU equivalent basis, one barrel of oil equals 7 to 8 gallons of natural gas. In other words, if oil were selling for $70 or $80 a barrel, then natural gas should be approximately $10 per MCF. The current price of natural gas is $3-4 per MCF, thus, it represents a tremendous bargain. Natural gas in Europe costs about $12 per MCF and in Japan it is over $15 per MCF. The reason for this discrepancy in pricing is because the natural gas markets are regional, while the oil markets are worldwide. Although there is some pricing advantage in oil in the U.S., it is much less than the advantage of natural gas pricing. While natural gas can be transported in liquefied form, this is a quite expensive process. As noted previously, the U.S. is now getting ready to export natural gas.

Natural gas used in vehicles is in gaseous form; it is under high pressure in specially built tanks. Natural gas cannot be converted to gasoline, but it can be converted to a form of diesel fuel. In some countries, natural gas is the primary fuel used for vehicles, but in the U.S. a substantial new infrastructure would be required in order to utilize natural gas for transportation. It is possible, however, to use the natural gas entering the home. In some states, this is being done. At this time, natural gas would cost approximately $2.00 per gallon of gas equivalent, or about 60% of the price of gasoline. If the infrastructure were put in place, the price per gallon of gas equivalent could be even lower.

It is somewhat surprising that environmentalists have taken such a negative position regarding natural gas. Natural gas is by far the cleanest of fossil fuels. Substitution of natural gas for coal in electrical generation has produced the sharpest drop in carbon emissions in the U.S.; far more than conversion to solar or wind. Nonetheless, environmentalists continue to oppose natural gas and have demonized the gas fracking process.

In the movie *Gasland,* for example, fracking was portrayed as having caused water from a faucet to catch on fire. In fact, the water already had natural gas in it. This was an intentionally fabricated story. While there could be some justification for opposing natural gas on the grounds that it could reduce the efforts to transition to solar and other non-fossil fuels, efforts to demonize the fracking process and the use of natural gas as a bridge fuel has been surprising.

T. Boone Pickens has been a tireless spokesman for the natural gas industry. He has referred to natural gas as a bridge fuel to a time when wind, solar, and other renewable fuels can be used to replace dirty fossil fuels. He has crusaded for the conversion of tractor trailers to run on natural gas. His crusade makes perfectly good sense from a practical standpoint, but it has gained very little traction.

Environmentalists

A local environmentalist and self-professed energy expert named David Roper is a good example of the extreme position that environmentalists have taken regarding natural gas. Mr. Roper is a retired physics professor from Virginia Tech who drives an electric car, a Nissan Leaf. Mr. Roper's views are frequently expressed in *The Roanoke Times*, our local newspaper, and the paper apparently agrees with his insistence that he is an energy expert since they give him so much ink. Mr. Roper goes through the standard litany of environmental objections to the natural gas boom, but he goes one step further. He states that he has *proof* that the natural gas boom will be a short lived phenomenon. I visited his web site to see what he was talking about. His "proof" is a mathematical model—a model developed by M. King Hubbert, a petroleum engineer who correctly predicted the peak in U.S. oil production. This mathematical model came to be known as Hubbert's Peak. Mr. Roper's model of U.S. natural gas production from the fracking process is temporary, primarily because fracking has been so successful. In effect, because the growth in natural gas has been so dramatic with the advent of fracking his model predicts that it will peak and suddenly decline. What troubles me about

Mr. Roper's assertions, and environmentalist complaints in general, is that they are so sure that their predictions will come to pass. As far as Mr. Roper's models are concerned, they did not predict the increased production of natural gas nor the increased production of oil in the U.S. But, nonetheless, he offers these models as *proof* that the natural gas phenomenon will be ephemeral. Let me state that there are reasons to be cautious regarding fracking, and in some cases, critical of the lack of transparency in the practices of certain companies involved in the fracking process. For example, the storage of waste water from the process is a problem. It can be injected back into the ground, which sometimes produces tremors or it can be placed in storage ponds. Either way, this obviously can be a problem. Also, some companies do not want to divulge the chemicals used in the fracking process because they feel they have an advantage in the particular makes of chemicals they are using and do not want the competition to know about it. However, I am convinced that the advantages of fracking far outweigh these disadvantages.

I do feel some grudging sympathy for environmentalists such as Mr. Roper. They believe they have the world all figured out. Fossil fuels would be phased out with a transition to wind, solar, and other renewables plus new technologies. Oil and natural gas in North America would be decreasing in volume and increasingly expensive. Consequently, they could use the fear of dependence on Middle Eastern oil as one of the primary reasons for a massive effort to switch to renewable energy. And, with the election of President Obama in 2008, they felt that everything was fitting into place for a miracle of renewable energy and electric cars. Thus, they made investments of hundreds of billions of dollars in companies like Solendra. First Solar, and other projects by the Obama Administration, would seal the deal. First Solar's stock exploded to a price of over $100. And, Solendra was touted as the vision of the future by President Obama.

All this came crashing down with the use of new techniques to produce oil and natural gas in the U.S. Solendra had a well-publicized bankruptcy and First Solar stock crashed to $20. But, what amazes me about Mr. Roper and others in the environmental movement is they won't recognize the change that has occurred.

More importantly, President Obama seems not to have made up his mind on the issue. After running in 2012 on an "all of the above" energy strategy, he lapsed back into declaring renewable energy from his '08 campaign as his plan in the inauguration speech. But, then in the State of the Union speech, he extolled the virtues of natural gas.

I do believe the pragmatic conclusion will prevail.

At its best, natural gas could be the bridge to the future. And it would give us time to do research to determine what that future would be. The implementation of solar and wind technology simply because it was available and "shovel ready" should be replaced by an emphasis on research efforts to determine what fuels make the most sense. Whether it is wind and solar, or fusion and hydrogen cars, natural gas will provide a bridge (time) to permit the research needed to see what makes the best sense for the future. In the concluding chapter, I will make the case that this is one of the efforts that President Obama should adopt in his effort to create jobs and economic growth.

Notes to myself

1. Van Jones became the green energy czar in the Obama Administration. Never mind that he knew practically nothing about energy.
2. We're extremely fortunate that the shale gas revolution was not entirely in the red states of Texas and Oklahoma. Had this been the case, I am cynical enough to believe that President Obama might well have made a different choice. But, the fact that natural gas production was increasing jobs in western Pennsylvania and eastern Ohio, where the economies were extremely weak and both were swing states, made the decision easier.
3. I do sympathize with the folks in West Virginia and the other coal producing areas. The sad towns in the coal producing areas are destined to be even sadder in the future as the production of natural gas increases.
4. Note: The cost of liquefying natural gas and transporting it to another country is around $5.00 per MCF. That is after the cost of converting the facility to liquefy the natural gas. This would allow U.S. natural gas to be sold at a lower rate than the current prices in Europe and certainly in Asia. Whereas, the European price is approximately $12.00 or $13.00 per MCF and the price in Asia is in the high teens.
5. Note: There were twenty-some facilities in the U.S. that were in some stage of construction to accept liquefied natural gas (LNG). They are now being converted or potentially could be converted to be used in exporting LNG.
6. Note: Liquefied natural gas have traditionally traded more akin to oil prices than to natural gas prices. However, with fracking, NGL prices have also come down. Butane, propane and ethane prices have all come down.
7. Note: Sixteen of the twenty-some facilities that were designed to import natural gas have now applied for a license to export natural gas. So far, only one has been approved. As to pricing, the break even cost of fracking is approximately $4.00—$4.50 per MCF. But, even at $5.00-6.00 per MCF, natural gas would be half the price of oil on a BTU equivalent basis.

8. Note: It is important to note that from a political standpoint, fracking was a job creator, not just in red states such as Texas and Oklahoma, but, also in western Pennsylvania and eastern Ohio which were among the contested states in the past election. Had this not been the case, it is hard to determine whether or not the political pressure would have been significant enough to sway the Obama Administration from allowing the EPA to slow the natural gas revolution or even to shut it down all together.

9. Note: The booming oil production from fracking has much less of an impact on oil prices than on natural gas prices. While there has been a 20% discount of U.S. oil to international oil prices, production in Bakken, ND and the Eagle Ford Shale in Texas are the only two areas which have increased production dramatically. There have been some positive reports in Ohio and West Virginia which show promise of development in the Marcellus Shale. However, they are largely inconclusive. California has a huge tract of very promising shale in the Monterey basin, but California is among the states with the most stringent regulations. The political climate in California makes potential fracking difficult to estimate.

I would like to take issue with David Roper's characterization of the U.S. energy situation. As a long term investor in energy companies, the U.S. is currently experiencing the most dramatic resurgence in oil and gas production in decades.

The recent growth in production of natural gas and oil is an extraordinary economic game changer. Mr. Roper claims to have proof that the natural gas boom is just a temporary flash in the pan. His "proof" is a mathematical model which fails to take into account the extraordinary change which is now occurring because of hydraulic fracturing or "fracking" and horizontal drilling.

Natural gas production in the U.S. has increased by 28% and oil production has increased by 50%. The price of both fuels is cheaper in the U.S. than any other industrialized country. In fact, natural gas prices fell below $2.00 per million BTUs several years ago before bouncing back to $3.50 per MBTU currently. In contrast, Europe is around $12.00 per MCF and Japan around $15.00 per MCF. This is producing an extraordinary economic boom in mid-America. To this point, the boom has primarily been in the exploration and production of natural gas, but increasingly this will produce dramatic job growth in industries such as chemicals, steel production, etc.

Why would we not celebrate this game changing event? To environmentalists such as Mr. Roper fracking is a dirty word. In fact though,

Energy Secretary Chu, has definitely concluded that fracking can be done safely. But, environmentalists are concerned that their neat picture of the world has fundamentally changed.

As with any major change, there will be some negative repercussions. For example, cheap natural gas is replacing some coal used in electrical generation. While this is sad for the coal miners, gas is much cleaner than coal. In fact, the reduction in CO2 emissions from natural gas replacing coal has been the most significant reduction in such emissions in history.

I also have some grudging sympathy for the environmentalists who thought that with Obama's election, wind and solar would have a dramatic effect on CO2 emissions. With their apt criticism of the imported oil and the planned importing of natural gas, they believed that this would create an environment where solar and wind would take over. But, despite the Obama Administration having spent billions of dollars on green energy, the impact on CO2 emissions has been far less than with the increased use of natural gas for electrical generation.

As a long term investor in natural gas, I would add a note of caution to potential investors. Most of the companies that have pioneered the natural gas revolution are small companies that are not well known. More importantly, these companies are a victim of their own success as natural gas has fallen from around $12.00 per million BTUs to the current price of around $3.50. This is not to say that there are not great investments in natural gas, but to this point they have been in support industries such as oil service companies, pipelines and increasingly in companies that will benefit from the cheaper prices, such as chemical companies.

A further benefit from the natural gas revolution will be in transportation. While Mr. Roper touts his electric car, the potential reduction in gasoline usage is an equally dramatic prospect in the future. While many countries have virtually all their vehicles running on natural gas, in the U.S. we have just scratched the surface. Honda manufactures an automobile which runs on natural gas. This car is not yet available in Virginia, but when it is, I hope to be one of the first purchasers. More seriously though, the biggest impact of natural gas as a transportation fuel will be in the replacement of diesel fuel in trucks.

The thing that bugs me about Mr. Roper's commentary on US energy is that he is so convinced of the accuracy of his beliefs on these complex issues. He pretends to be an expert with no proof of his beliefs. Further, we should be celebrating the economic game-changer fracking that has been. I hope Mr. Roper and other environmentalists will take a fresh, objective view of the tremendous benefits of the natural gas revolution in the U.S.

Chapter Nine

Some Concluding Comments

Despite some of the negative trends cited in this book, it is important to note that the world is in a better position now than it has been in any time in its history. The number of people living below the poverty level in China has been reduced dramatically in recent years. The internet has already changed everything, and will continue to make dramatic changes in the future. While I am still amazed that a technician in India can take over my office PC to update some function, this will become a common place in the future and our kids will think nothing of it. The world has become an open society with only North Korea, Iran, Syria and a few others trying to buck the trend.

While the proceeding comments will provide little comfort to a 55-year-old laid off textile worker in South Carolina, or a coal miner in West Virginia or the furniture manufacturers in Martinsville, VA, these trends are extremely important to note.

For President Obama, it will soon be time for him to be concerned about his legacy. In foreign affairs, I believe, his legacy will be solid. In the Middle East, Iran remains the biggest question mark of his second term. He will be credited with ending two wars there, although the war in Iraq was already being wound down. I do not believe he will be involved in any other Middle Eastern military conflict. In retrospect, his Cairo speech was too optimistic, but it was a heartfelt view of the way things could be in the Middle East.

He has been very adroit in fighting the more extreme elements of the Muslim regimes without engaging a full scale military effort. The drone strikes against extremist leaders have been very successful. He successfully used a quick strike capability to kill Osama Bin Laden and seems to have affectively turned the CIA into a paramilitary organization. Perhaps most importantly, he will have restored America to seeking peace and democracy around the world. I believe the Obama administration has made considerable progress opening up the closed society in North Korea and in restoring a more normal relationship with Cuba.

On the domestic side, I believe his legacy is destined to be more mixed. The biggest question at this point is the winding down of the bond bubble and the accumulation of a tremendous amount of new debt. It appears the federal debt will be almost doubled from $11 trillion to over $20 trillion in his eight years in office. It remains to be seen whether this huge increase in debt can be absorbed without triggering a period of rapid inflation or deflation.

One of these allusions of Keynesian economics that is practiced in the U.S. is that it can be used to stimulate the economy with no negative consequences.

Milton Friedman's favorite axiom "There is no such thing as a free lunch."

What Obama should do now?

If I had the opportunity to discuss the economic initiatives for the next three and a half years with President Obama, I would recommend that first: *he recognize that the protracted economic weakness in the economies of the U.S., the European Union, and Japan are primarily structural in nature stemming from globalization.* The huge increase in the labor force, primarily from China, presents an unprecedented problem. In the U.S., this has resulted in almost two decades of stagnant compensation for the middle and lower middle class workers. The federal government should do whatever possible to encourage economic growth and to reduce unemployment.

This means working with companies to encourage hiring more U.S. workers and working with foreign companies to try to get them to move manufacturing to the U.S. When President Obama spoke of creating a Department of Business during the campaign, this was a rational approach that was derided by the Republicans. However, short of creating a new department, the Commerce Department could take on this role. With the new Commerce Secretary being a longtime friend and backer of President Obama, Ms. Penny Pritzker could lead the charge to attempt to get companies to increase their job base in the U.S.

The former head of Intel, Paul Otellini, says that any country that they would invest in would offer them tax breaks, a financial package, an ombudsman to reduce red tape, etc.—except for the United States. This has got to change. Just like states compete now for companies to build plants in their area, the federal government must do what other governments around the world already do.

I emphasize this working with companies as opposed to federal government intervention in stimulating the economy, because Congress may not approve the stimulating measures and the federal deficit is already too high.

Second, *embrace natural gas and North American energy independence.* I discussed in the last chapter the revolution occurring in natural gas production. This results in U.S. natural gas of about one third of the cost of natural gas in Europe and Asia. This is an extraordinary advantage.

I would suggest that President Obama visit one of the LNG import terminals being converted to export terminals. The next pending approval is for the Cove Point terminal in the Chesapeake Bay; he could visit this by helicopter from the White House. This would emphasize that companies have spent millions of dollars creating import terminals which are now being converted into export terminals because U.S. natural gas has increased so dramatically and unexpectedly. I think the president should admit that he was no fan of natural gas production when he became president, but that hydraulic fracturing has proved to be a safe way to increase natural gas production and that the U.S. has an incredible cost advantage versus other countries. He could follow this up by visiting one of the steel plants being built on the Ohio River by European countries.

Third, *foreign relations*: it is likely that the Middle East will continue to occupy an inordinate amount of the President's time. This is especially unfortunate in economic terms because the world's economic growth will increasingly trend toward Asia. Afghanistan will probably not end well. And the revolution that is occurring in various countries from Egypt to Syria will get rid of dictators, but will likely be replaced by fundamentalist Islamic regimes. In some cases it will be a matter of going from one form of dictatorship to another. Iraq and Iran will continue to be problems. I believe the U.S. policy should be to try to reduce the time and effort spent on the Middle East—gradually turning things over to a consortium in the area and a group headed by the U.S. involving NATO and the United Nations. This will not be easy, but it is the best prospect to achieve a semblance of order. If a peaceful containment strategy can be executed, this will permit some economic progress and social progress in various countries.

Fourth, *the role of education*: I think education is very difficult to deal with in summary fashion. In the U.S., the role of a college education has gotten a great deal attention. Statistics emphasize the income differential of a high school graduate versus a high school dropout; and a college education versus a high school education. However, while these statistics are accurate, they do not deal with the disparity in the various degrees of income relative to a student's major in college. In fact, with certain majors, students are having a tough time finding a job, much less having an income differential that is positive relative to high school graduates.

Anyone who writes the "fate of the world" book feels the need to put in an obligatory chapter on the role of education in saving the world. I have not done that because I think education is really a mixed message. Students who are going deep into debt with student loans to get a degree in psychology or fine arts will probably not recover their investment. Conversely, going into debt to receive a degree in engineering or medicine is perfectly logical. This has been recognized with the emphasis on the STEM courses—science, technology, engineering and mathematics. The percent of U.S. students majoring in these subjects decreased dramatically over the recent years.

My primary recommendation to President Obama would be to enhance the internet education offerings. As more and more professors have begun to make lectures available on the internet, the federal government could play a key role in making these courses available perhaps through MOOCS— massive open online courses—that could be offered through community colleges. This would enable any student to get access to the best professors in the world, and have the community college setting as a forum for discussion of the issues, and a teacher who would facilitate that discussion. This would greatly reduce the need for students to borrow funds, as well as enhancing their educational benefit.

Don's Reading List

John A. Allison
The Financial Crisis and the Free Market Cure: Why Pure Capitalism is the World Economy's Only Hope

Sheila Bair
Bull by the Horns: Fighting to Save Main Street from Wall Street and Wall Street from Itself

Donald L. Barlett and James B. Steele
The Betrayal of the American Dream

Dr. William J. Bennett and David Wilezol
Is College Worth It?: A Former United States Secretary of Education and a Liberal Arts Graduate Expose the Broken Promise of Higher Education

Ben S. Bernanke
The Federal Reserve and the Financial Crisis

Bill Bishop
The Big Sort: Why the Clustering of Like-Minded America is Tearing Us Apart

Alan S. Blinder
After the Music Stopped: The Financial Crisis, the Response, and the Work Ahead

John C. Bogle
The Clash of the Cultures: Investment vs. Speculation

L. Brent Bozell III & Tim Graham
Collusion: How the Media Stole the 2012 Election and How to Stop Them from Doing it in 2016

Donald M. Kinzer

Jeb Bush and Clint Bolick
Immigration Wars: Forging and American Solution

Robert Bryce
Power Hungry: The Myths of "Green" Energy and the Real Fuels of the Future

Bill Clinton
Back to Work: Why We Need Smart Government for a Strong Economy

Tom A. Coburn with John Hart
The Debt Bomb: A Bold Plan to Stop Washington From Bankrupting America

Michael K. Farr
Restoring Our American Dream: The Best Investment

Noah Feldman
Cool War: The Future of Global Competition

Chrystia Freeland
Plutocrats: The Rise of the New Global Super-Rich and the Fall of Everyone Else

Thomas L. Friedman
Hot, Flat, and Crowded: Why We Need a Green Revolution—And How it Can Renew America
That Used To Be Us: How America Fell Behind in the World it Invented and How We Can Come Back
The World is Flat: A Brief History of the Twenty-First Century

Alan C. Greenberg
The Rise and Fall of Bear Stearns

Alan Greenspan
The Map and the Territory: Risk, Human Nature, and the Future of Forecasting

Richard N. Haass
Foreign Policy Begins at Home: The Case for Putting America's House in Order

Jacob S. Hacker & Paul Pierson
Winner-Take-All: Politics: How Washington Made the Rich Richer—And Turned Its Back on the Middle Class

Greg Ip
The Little Book of Economics: How the Economy Works in the Real World

Van Jones
Rebuild the Dream

Robert D. Kaplan
The Revenge of Geography

Charles P. Kindleberger and Robert Aliber
Manias, Panics, and Crashes: A History of Financial Crisis, 5th ed.

Russel Kinnel
FundSpy: Morningstar's Inside Secrets to Selecting Mutual Funds That Outperform

Edward Klein
The Amateur: Barack Obama in the White House

Dr. Richard G. Lee
The Coming Revolution: Signs from America's Past That Signal Our Nation's Future

Richard G. Lipsey & Peter O. Steinner
Economics

Peter Lynch
One Up On Wall Street: How to Use Who You Already Know to Make Money in the Market

Thomas E. Mann and Norman J. Ornstein
It's Even Worse Than it Looks: How the American Constitutional System Collided with the New Politics of Extremism

John J. Mearsheimer and Stephen M. Watt
The Israel Lobby and U.S. Foreign Policy

Duff McDonald
Last Man Standing: The Ascent of Jamie Dimon and JPMorgan Chase

Gretchen Morgenson and Joshua Rosner
Reckless Endangerment: How Outsized Ambition, Greed, and Corruption Led to Economic Armageddon

Donald M. Kinzer

Andrew P. Morriss, William T. Bogart, Roger E. Meiners, and Andrew Dorchak
The False Promise of Green Energy

Helaine Olen
Pound Foolish: Exposing the Dark Side of the Personal Finance Industry

George Packer
The Unwinding: An Inner History of the New America

Robert B. Reich
Beyond Outrage: What Has Gone Wrong with Our Economy and Our Democracy, and How to Fix It

Carmen M. Reinhart & Kenneth S. Rogoff
This Time is Different: Eight Centuries of Financial Folly

Ed Rendell
A Nation of Wusses: How America's Leaders Lost the Guts to Make US Great

Jim Rogers
Street Smarts: Adventures on the Road and in the Markets

Larry Schweikart
48 Liberal Lies About American History (That You Probably Learned in School)

Peter D. Schiff
The Real Crash: How to Save Yourself and Your Country

Edmond J. Siefried
Economics for Bankers

Jeremy J. Siegel
Stocks for the Long Run: The Definitive Guide to Financial Market Returns and Long-Term Investment Strategies, 3rd edition

William L. Silber
Volcker: The Triumph of Persistence

Nate Silver
The Signal and the Noise: Why so Many Predictions Fail—But Some Don't

Hedrick Smith
Who Stole the American Dream?

David A. Stockman
The Great Deformation: The Corruption of Capitalism in America

Arvind Subramanian
Eclipse: Living in the Shadow of China's Economic Dominance

Evan Thomas
Ike's Bluff: President Eisenhower's Secret Battle to Save the World

David M. Walker
Comeback America: Turning the Country Around and Restoring Fiscal Responsibility

Juan Williams
Muzzled: The Assault on Honest Debate

Bob Woodward
The Price of Politics

Daniel Yergin
The Quest: Energy, Security, and the Remaking of the Modern World

Fareed Zakaria
The Post-American World

Don Kinzer spent most of his professional life in investments and financial management. He worked at Dominion Bankshares/First National Exchange and Shenandoah Life Insurance Company. He taught financial courses at Hollins University and Roanoke College. Don was an avid tennis player, a student of investment markets, and enjoyed a good Budweiser.

Don believed the economic and financial markets have missed the key event holding back world growth: globalization. Globalization unleashed over one billion consumers and workers with the fall of the Berlin wall in 1990. The subsequent decline in communism was an historical economic event which had both positive and negative elements. The most negative element for the developed world was the limits on growth which are thus limiting employment. As the developed world has tried to maintain its lifestyle, even with the slower growth, it has resorted to more and more debt. Many advanced countries are now approaching historically dangerous debt levels. The resolution of this struggle between developed and developing countries will prove whether globalization has been a positive or negative force.

www.ingramcontent.com/pod-product-compliance
Lightning Source LLC
Chambersburg PA
CBHW050431290526
45786CB00003B/1486